Chad,

Thank you [for your]
service. May the angels
of the Lord encamp round
about you to keep you safe!

Danny Lippinel

Beef Stew for Cops

...and for those who know one

Danny Lynchard

iUniverse, Inc.
New York   Bloomington

Beef Stew for Cops
...and for those who know one

iUniverse books may be ordered through booksellers or by contacting:

iUniverse
1663 Liberty Drive
Bloomington, IN 47403
www.iuniverse.com
1-800-Authors (1-800-288-4677)

*Because of the dynamic nature of the Internet, any Web addresses or links contained in this book
may have changed since publication and may no longer be valid.*

ISBN: 978-1-4502-1191-8 (sc)
ISBN: 978-1-4502-1192-5 (ebk)

Printed in the United States of America

iUniverse rev. date: 4/15/2010

BEEF STEW FOR COPS

"God supplies the paint for the silver lining in every cloud. It is often applied, however, by the most unlikely of hands. Someone must be willing to step inside our uncertainties and with sincerity, commitment, and professionalism, paint the beauty. Some of them wear a uniform."

- Chaplain Danny Lynchard, Author

"Skillfully written, definitely written from the hand and heart of someone who has been there, Reverend Lynchard's "Beef Stew for Cops" offers a unique perspective into the trauma and crisis faced by those beneath the badge – yet allows for a new perspective from the Mighty Counselor and a healing touch right from the Master's hand."

- Rev., Dr. Charles Lorrain, Director
The International Conference of Police Chaplains

"Fire fighting is about more than putting out fires. It is about the lives affected by fire. It's the reason we climb aboard a fire engine and walk into the flames. Chaplain Lynchard's book captures the fortitude, the risk, and more importantly, the people involved when the sirens scream. "

Fire Chief Alan La Croix
Tulsa, OK

"I am proud to call Rev. Lynchard a colleague, friend, and personal advisor. The collection of spiritual thoughts he provides to the reader in his collective work on the police profession are indicative of his dedication and sacrifice made on behalf of the Tulsa Police Department for the citizens of Tulsa for over two decades. His insights are an uncommon, accurate portrayal of those difficult questions posed to law enforcement, which only faith can answer."

Police Chief Ron Palmer
Tulsa, OK

"Chaplain Lynchard's devotional provides a unique perspective to the reader of what we in law enforcement live every day."

- Police Chief Richard Easley, 1974-2004
Kansas City, MO

"No one can ever know the psychological effects of this profession without having personally experienced the drama and tension confronted by police officers. Reverend Lynchard captures the very essence of the range of these emotions and presents them in a fashion that causes one to pause and reflect on life's experiences."

-Police Chief Tom Streicher
Cincinnati, Ohio

"Reverend Lynchard's stories capture the difficult and emotional encounters that can only be understood by those who share the law enforcement profession. It's a "chicken soup for cops" that brings peace and meaning to a job that few people understand – even those who work in it."

- Police Chief Robert McNeilly, 1997-2007
Pittsburgh, OH

For nearly twenty years, I have known, worked with and observed Reverend Danny Lynchard provide his unassuming, compassionate, and timely spiritual support to police officers and fire fighters. His collection of stories about their work and resulting personal struggles provides a reader unique insight into the lives of men and women who so generously serve others. Reverend Lynchard's stories combine the wisdom of experience with spiritual messages for living a balanced life.

M. Susan Savage
Oklahoma Secretary of State
Former Mayor of Tulsa

ACKNOWLEDGEMENTS

My thanks to my wife, Susan Lynchard, whose love and devotion have made a home where life is always good and God is always close.

And to Carol Mersch, whose persistence and foresight made this tribute to police and firefighters everywhere possible.

ABOUT THE AUTHOR

Danny Lynchard

Danny Lynchard was ordained as a Baptist Minister at age twenty and has been in the ministry for more than thirty years. He is a licensed private pilot and the Director of the Tulsa Police/Fire Chaplaincy Corps, where he has served for over twenty years. In this capacity he oversees numerous volunteer chaplains who work with 1000+ law enforcement and firefighter personnel. He directly observes investigations and has personally dealt with over 1000 families during times of catastrophic grief. His chaplaincy role has placed him in the living rooms of virtually every faith in America. His extensive involvement in virtually every aspect of law enforcement has provided him with a good working knowledge of some of the latest forensic and investigative procedures.

He is a freelance writer for several Christian publications and is co-author of a military devotional, *Coming Home: For Those Who Serve and Those Who Wait*. He and his wife, Susan, live on the outskirts of Tulsa.

CONTENTS

FOREWORD

The situations and events often faced by law enforcement officers encompass a wide range of emotions. Reverend Lynchard's thoughts and insightful observations provide a refreshing perspective of our not so perfect world. He reminds us that even in tragic circumstances, faith in God and in our humanity can bring about a true sense of peace. He understands the essence of being a police officer and the responsibilities it carries.

Beef Stew for Cops is not your typical "cop story"…it's much more. True, telling and inspirational. A collection of stories that captures the real meaning of being a police officer. The highs, the lows, the whole range of emotions that every police officer experiences. A must read for both the professional and the general public alike.

Reverend Lynchard has written a truly inspirational book. He knows the emotional impact of "being on the job". *Beef Stew for Cops* provides a sense of direction and purpose to those tough situations faced by all law enforcement officers. It's not only good reading, it captures the real meaning of being a police officer.

- John Walsh
Assistant Director, National Center for Emergency Preparedness
Vanderbilt University

TO THE READER

The stories you read here are true. As Director of Chaplaincy of the Police and Fire Departments of a major city for more than twenty five years it has been my duty to help the hurting get through some of the toughest times of their lives. I've dealt with the bad guys, the good guys, and the God guys. They have marked my life forever.

Out of appreciation for their humble service, dates of events have been removed and names changed in respect of the individuals involved and in order for the true message of the story to shine through.

I purposely chose to take you deeper than reality television so that you may see the gold in the gutter and among the glitter.

1

When the Glory Doesn't Glitter

Tuesday, February 5, 7:00 p.m.

As we drove slowly by the small two-bedroom home with white siding and black shutters, the officer suddenly pulled the police cruiser up into the entrance. It was 7:00 p.m. and already dark in Tulsa.

"Her car is here. I've been trying to serve this warrant for receiving stolen property since three o'clock this afternoon."

As we walked up the driveway, I counted four dogs—none of them willing to rise from their rest to alert the unsuspecting tenants of our arrival. My heart began to pump harder as the excitement of arresting the "bad guy" began to build. I expected a heavily bearded, tattooed, leather-wearing boyfriend to open the door. Instead, a blue-eyed, blond haired, three-year-old boy, dressed in Mickey Mouse pajamas greeted us with excitement and shouted, "Mom, Grammaw, a policeman has come to see us!"

I stood quietly as the officer informed the little boy's mother that she would need to come with us to the booking area of the police station.

"I promise I didn't know all those things were stolen," she said repeatedly.

"Yes, Ma'am," said the officer, "but you're still going to have to go with me. I can't make the decisions you want me to make. That's for a judge and jury to decide."

I watched as a child's innocent blue eyes came to the frightening conclusion that his mom would be going to jail. He began to cry. "Please don't take my Momma to jail, Mr. Policeman. I need my Momma. Please don't take her with you. I'm supposed to sleep with her tonight ... in her bed!"

The sight of little hands with dimples where knuckles ought to be, clenching the green stripe on the officer's uniformed trousers was, indeed, heart wrenching. He screamed even louder.

"Please, please, Mister Policeman, please let my Momma stay here with me. I need my Momma. I get scared at night without her!"

Neither I nor his grandmother could console him. Our assurance that mom would be fine and could make bail by morning did nothing to resolve his fear and grief. The officer seemed unaffected...until we got in the car. "Damn, I hate this job, sometimes." He turned to his prisoner and said, "If you were half a decent mother, I wouldn't have to do this!"

I understood his outburst. Her haphazard, self-centered lifestyle had inflicted this uncomfortable, distasteful task on us. We wanted to be the good guys. We didn't feel like it at all.

<hr/>

Silver Bullet: When we do what is right, even when it feels wrong, we become the only thing that stands between freedom and anarchy. Do what is right. Season it with mercy and let God work all things for good.

Shield: "And he went a little further, and fell on his face, and prayed, saying, O my Father, if it be possible, let this cup pass from me: nevertheless not as I will, but as thou wilt." Matt 26:39

Prayer: Lord, comfort those I cannot. Help them see I have a job to do. Comfort me when my task becomes unpleasant and help me remember that you care more for the hurting than even I do.

2

Sometimes the Sword

Saturday, May 19, 1:00 a.m.

Acting on a tip, officers sat discreetly in unmarked vehicles surrounding an all-night eating establishment. This case would make great headlines. If the tip was accurate, the officers would soon bring a string of robberies and rapes to an end. The plan was simple. Wait until the suspect arrived to rob the establishment, move as a group, identify yourself as police officers, and take the suspect into custody. Then simply enjoy the headlines you create by bringing the crime spree to an end.

Right on time, a van pulled close to the establishment and an average-sized man in an overcoat stepped out of the passenger door. He walked briskly into the restaurant, pulled a shotgun from behind his back and demanded money. He took the money and stepped outside. Several voices yelled, "Police Officers!! Throw down your weapon and get on the ground!"

Instead, he turned and headed back into the building.

Seconds later a young policeman sat on the curb, eyes focused down at the concrete as if to be reading some sort of message in the ripples of the pavement. It was so quiet now. Only moments ago the soft evening breeze was pierced by the boom of a six-shot revolver sending .357 projectiles down a four inch grooved barrel and into the chest of the stranger at a velocity faster than the speed of sound. His life left him just that fast. He had trained for this event all of his career, yet never believed it would happen. If only he had thrown down his weapon. If only he had not tried to turn back into the restaurant and possibly take hostages. If only, if only. In a split second the decision had to be made: Terminate the threat. Fancy words for taking a life. The tension and stress were so high that the officer never even heard the shots that bolted the neighborhood awake.

It was quiet now. Only the ringing in his ears, the smell of gunpowder, the light powder burns across the right index knuckle, and, of course, the limp body in the doorway revealed that something traumatic had just happened. Maybe that's why the Colt six-shooter was called the "Peace Maker." The eerie noiselessness after the blast was deafening.

But there was no peace in this young officer's heart. He had just taken a life. It was necessary, he thought. It had to be done.

As the night became morning, he took a shower, and, as was his Sunday morning custom, he left for his Sunday Bible class.

~~~

Silver Bullet: In the times when it seems God could not possibly be present, He still promises to never leave or forsake you.

Shield: "For he is the minister of God to thee for good. But if thou do that which is evil, be afraid; for he beareth not the sword in vain: for he is the minister of God, a revenger to execute wrath upon him that doeth evil." Romans 13:4

Prayer: Father, may I never have to fire my weapon against my fellow man. Give me Your wisdom to see every other avenue. But should that decision become my lot, for the sake of my family, my fellow officers, and my community, keep my mind clear, my hand steady, and my aim sure.

3

Facing Fear by Faith

Friday, August 17, 11:30 a.m.

Most residential fires start in the wintertime. Families break out the old space heaters, fire up the fireplaces, light up the coal oil heaters or gas furnaces, and the opportunity for ignition skyrockets. This particular home fire was different. Not only was it during the hottest month of the summer, August, but it was actually started by firefighters.

The rookie class met early in the morning and stood out front of the house with a drawing board and several instructors to discuss the best way to start and extinguish a house fire. A local builder had donated the old home for a training exercise. It was a rare opportunity for firefighters to practice what they had learned in a controlled environment. None, however, knew of the spiritual lesson that would be taught to a seven-year-old girl standing on the perimeter.

Word had gotten out to the neighborhood and people began to arrive as early as nine o'clock to watch the exercise. Even the news media arrived in their brightly painted vans with reporters and camera crews to film the event.

It was an older brick home with deteriorating white trim. All the windows were still intact and the shingled green roof appeared to have a few more good years ahead of it...but not much more. There were several huge trees in the yard. Their safety took up a lot of the planning time before igniting the residence could take place. The sun lifted higher and higher into the sky and the temperature soared toward the one hundred degree mark.

Three times during the day, the house was set on fire. Each time in a different location, with different accelerants and circumstances. Each time the brave men and women put on the heavy fire retardant clothing, oxygen tanks and gear, entered the building, and extinguished the flame. It was now three o'clock in the afternoon and time to burn it completely down.

To prevent the fire from spreading, firefighters were positioned at various locations around the building. Each of them held a fire hose that would throw a stream of water high above the residence and beyond its perimeter. Now it appeared the whole neighborhood was there for the big event.

I stood along the roadway without saying much to anyone around. A few feet in front of me stood a family of four. Mom held an infant while her seven-year-old daughter stood beside her with dad. She was such a tiny little thing, with light brown hair that fell just below her shoulder and in her shiny brown eyes. She stood on one foot and then the other as she watched the fire begin to show itself through the bedroom window.

The fire was small at first, with a lot of thick gray smoke pouring out of the roof and around the eves. As it grew in intensity, one could see the flames leaping up to reveal themselves from the back of the house. A large bush of some sort grew against the left side of the nonresident residence. It covered the entire side of the house and seemed to be huddled close as if seeking protection. Suddenly the fire was there! Everywhere! Like a large dragon it came to life with a roar, raised its ugly head above the roof and belched flames ten to twenty feet over the top of the residence. Had there been any conversation, the pops and cracks of the bush and other materials being brutally devoured would have easily drowned it out.

I was resting on my left foot with my right knee raised. The ferociousness of the flame seemed to take my breath. The little girl in front of me screamed, turned, and ran directly into my arms. She held onto my neck with little arms that belied the strength with which she held me in her grasp. She cried and screamed, "Don't let it get me! Don't let it get me!"

I was shocked to have a strange little girl run into my arms. It took a second to realize what had happened. The noise and sight of something raring up in front of her so quickly had frightened her to the point of running, even to a stranger, for comfort. Over and over again I spoke assuredly that nothing would get her.

As she began to believe me she eased her grip. "Are you sure? Who's going to stop it?"

Slowly I was able to turn her around and show her the firefighters positioned at strategic points around the house. They had released the water from the hoses and had tamed the fire to a safe level. "They are, sweetie." I said to her. "God has placed those firefighters between you and the fire. They are not going to let it get past them."

Bullet: Sometimes we may not realize until we look with the enlightened eyes of faith that God has been protecting us all along.

Shield: "I will encamp by my house as a guard that none may pass to and fro; No oppressor shall pass over them again, for now I have regard for their affliction." Zechariah .9: 8

Prayer: Lord, you are my guard and my shield. Sometimes you place me to represent you as a guard against things that hurt. Help me to see through the eyes of faith that You are with me. Help me to remain strong and steadfast so that others are safe behind me.

4

Practicing the Presence

Saturday, April 22, 9:30 p.m.

Dave Dunson is one of the truest people I know. Almost thirty years in the ministry have afforded me the opportunity to meet hundreds of ministers. None, however, has surpassed Dave in integrity, sincerity, and commitment. When Timothy McVeigh and associates decided to blow up the Murrah Building in Oklahoma City, I knew we could send no finer chaplain than Dave.

The scenes of smoke, rubble, debris, and troubled faces filled with fear only scratched the surface of the emotional turmoil that boiled inside the victims, firefighters, police officers, paramedics, and construction workers that became part of that catastrophe. In the first few hours and days, the number of dead continued to rise. Everyone wanted to help. Professional and nonprofessional people from all over the United States descended with open hands and hearts on Oklahoma City. Initially there was great hope in saving lives trapped under the ruins. Slowly many of the workers became aware that rescue was no longer an appropriate word to describe the task at hand.

A makeshift morgue was set up in one of the churches. For awhile, the line of National Guardsman bringing body bags holding body parts seemed nonstop. Dogs, brought in to find victims still alive, found so few living and so many dead they actually became depressed and refused to work anymore. Rescuers had to hide among the fallen boulders and allow the dogs to find them in order to keep the animals motivated enough to continue.

Then the rains came and the night became cold and wet. Dust turned to mud while floodlights illuminated the recovery area. The drone of bulldozers, tractors, and various other heavy equipment, filled the night air with a constant racket of rocks moving and engines revving. Faces, weary with fatigue and knitted into solemn gazes, seemed say, I'm no longer thinking. I'm just trying to get this done.

Into this scene stepped Dave. His clothes were clean. His appearance well kept. All of it looking much out of place in such a dismal area. Work went on all around him. He wore a white construction hard hat. On the front of the hard hat was a single highly polished gold cross. Every time he moved his head to change the direction of his glance, the tiny two-inch cross glistened in the light.

He stood there for a long time feeling quite out of place, yet honored to be a part of this great effort. Under his breath he prayed for those he saw working and wished he could do more. They were weary from the work and lack of success in finding people still alive after so long a time. Where was God? Where was the extra strength these wonderful people needed to carry on their work?

Quite unexpectedly the foreman of the work crew came over to Chaplain Dave. "Chaplain, do you think you could offer a prayer for me and these people out here?" he shouted over the noise of the equipment.

Knowing he could not be heard, Dave nodded in affirmation, thinking this man wanted him to remain in silent prayer for them. To Dave's surprise, that was not what he wanted at all. The foreman motioned to all the equipment operators to stop the engines of their machinery. One by one the massive machines became quiet, making everyone focus their attention on the head of operations.

He motioned every worker to his location and in a booming voice said, "I've asked the chaplain here to pray for us. I thought each of you would want to hear it."

In a reverence unsurpassed by any church service in America, each worker removed his hat, bowed his head and waited on Dave to pray.

I can't tell you what Dave prayed. I'm not so sure the words were that important. The miracle happened before the first words were ever uttered. Each person received a sense of divine calling during those next few moments. Somehow, God was counting on them to find bodies so families could mourn and get on with their life. They found value in what they were doing.

"Thanks, chaplain," said the large-framed foreman.

With that, everyone returned to work. The bulldozers and draglines fired up their massive diesel engines and each one worked with renewed determination and purpose.

Silver Bullet: Sometimes we don't need a change in jobs, just an insight into the good it accomplishes. Sometimes our purpose may change. That doesn't mean the new one isn't just as valid.

Shield: "Only fear the Lord, and serve him in truth with all your heart: for consider how great things he hath done for you." I Samuel 12:24

Prayer: Lord, when my way grows tired and I cannot see the good I am accomplishing, show me Your purpose so that I may find new strength and new joy.

5

The True Story Behind the Famous Photograph

Wednesday, April 19, 9:06 a.m.

Everyone in emergency service knows about the running competition between firefighters and police officers. As director of the police and fire chaplaincy corps, I have often felt like a soldier walking the Mason Dixon line wearing a gray coat and blue trousers. Admittedly the competition among them wasn't that bad, but it was always fun to listen to the complaining.

Police cars always set up the perimeter around the fire trucks. The idea is to keep the citizenry at a safe distance and out of the way of working firefighters. Those minutes after the fire is extinguished, the hoses rolled up, and the gear is being stacked up around the trucks, are times for some of the best bantering. After a long firefight, exhausted firefighters converse with cops who need to purge their bladders. The joking seems to help ease the frustration on both parts.

"You firemen have it made," says one police officer. "When the police get called to a scene and arrest the bad guy, half the people hate us and the other half wish we didn't have to come. You guys show up, break out the windows, chop holes in the roof, soak everything in the house, and drive away with people thinking you're heroes!"

Then, inevitably, one of the firefighters quips back, "Yeah, but the city loves you more. Look who always gets the most rookies, the best equipment, and the most television shows!"

The battle for more funding, pay increases, and the never-ending search for more equipment and better training manages to keep competition keen. But don't be fooled. Beneath this exterior of superficial conflict are hearts that beat the same. Behind all the patented answers you will find the desire to serve as protectors and lifesavers to be a motivating factor in each of their lives. The bombing of the William H. Murrah building in Oklahoma City was a case in point.

When the middle-aged Oklahoma City police officer went to work that morning, it was like hundreds, even thousands of days before. The squad meeting was light and jovial. The typical joking and jibing was all part of the roll call. In the same area of town, one of the city firefighters was lounging around the station house waiting for the first call of the day. Sometimes the calls were actually humorous. It is strange why some people will call for a fire truck. This day would change his life forever.

As the minute hand ticked past nine o'clock, a huge blast would rock the city. The impact of the blast would break windows for blocks away. Smoke would belch down the city streets and one hundred and sixty-eight people would die. Many of them would be children. The police radio cracked incessantly. The alarms went off in firehouses all over town. Now, together, police cars, ambulances, and fire trucks would drive together into the battle while hundreds of civilians ran away. True heroes working together to save a community.

Many people will remember the moving photograph of an Oklahoma City firefighter. His face solemn, sweaty, and dirty as he brought a little child out of the smoke and dust. His big hands and coat seemed to envelope the tiny body as wee legs dangled across his arms. A small innocent face was pressed up against his chest.

What many people never realized was that just a few seconds before that photo was taken, the little body was pulled from the rubble by a middle-aged policeman, placed in the hands of a firefighter, and taken to the paramedics who manned their stations with unequalled commitment. At that moment it was not about pay, equipment, manpower, or public exposure. It was about getting a little child out of the rubble and into a place of care.

There were no jokes, no competition, and no jealousy. Just gut-wrenching love in action.

Silver Bullet: The call to service must always be greater than the servant. The nobility of the task should never be diminished by the smallness of a prideful attitude.

Shield: "That they all may be one; as thou, Father, art in me, and I in thee, that they also may be one in us: that the world may believe that thou hast sent me." John 17:21

Prayer: Lord, let my calling be more important than my worries and personal gain. May I always see that true gain comes by Your hand and not by the accolades of comrades.

6

Broken but Unbeatable

Monday, July 12, 1:30 p.m.

Cheryl represented forty two years of life at its toughest. The bright sun bouncing off the white concrete parking lot seemed to carve the wrinkles even deeper into her face. The dark cloud hovering over her life had simply split apart and settled in each eye, giving her a gaunt, sleep-deprived appearance. Long, curly, disheveled brown hair rested on the shoulders of her blue uniform. Her clothes seemed to stay in place while her small frame drooped inside them. She had a hard time making eye contact. I remember thinking, were I to draw a picture of victimization, she would be the likeness.

This middle-aged lady stood in the parking lot, folding bloody clothes into a blue Wal-Mart shopping bag. "Will you please get rid of them? I can't seem to do it on my own."

It seemed odd that such an event would take place in a huge parking area in front of one of the largest grocery stores in town. The bizarre transaction made the whole normal-acting world seem out of sync. How did she wind up here, stuffing her boyfriend's blood soaked clothes into a plastic bag?

The sexual abuse began when she was three years old and continued until age eleven. Her father was the first perpetrator. It was the beginning of an education that continued to drive home the point, "If it wasn't my fault, I was at least an accomplice or mostly responsible." It was also the beginning of living with two-sided individuals. Men who revealed one side for public view and a dark, sinister side for which she alone was made privy.

To Cheryl, this is what love was. Love meant taking the blame and the beatings no matter who was at fault. Until today, she had lived the life of a perfect victim. She could be abused, misused, tormented, beaten, and belittled. Yet she would find a way to be the one at fault and keep the deep dark secret tucked inside any number of the cavernous scars furrowed across her heart.

She had been married and divorced repeatedly until the feeling anyone would love her at all was enough to merit her devotion. So at age 32, she and her son moved in with Steve. Like all the other relationships, it began with great promise. Steve worked hard, played hard, and drank hard. But he always included Cheryl. I guess its good to have someone around to blame when things go wrong -- or a human pillow with which to vent the depression and anger. Six months into this ten-year relationship the beatings began. Light at first, then heavier as the years marched on. Threats of "I'm going to kill you." were followed by extreme sorrow, empty promises, false blame, and repetition of the cycle.

August 31st marked the date of the final beating. It was a bad one. The first punch split the skin above her left eye and the side of her face became shiny red from the flow of blood. The second blow broke her nose. Her face and neck were now covered with the life-giving liquid. Believe it or not, it would be the very thing that saved her life.

Over and over he yelled, "I am going to kill you!" Blow after blow pounded into her small frame. Each one designed to prevent her from lifting hands and arms to protect her self. Slamming her into the floor he tried repeatedly to grab her in such a way as to break her neck or strangle her in order to terminate her existence. The blood on her face and neck simply made it too slippery to maintain a proper grasp.

Somehow during the punishment she was able to dial 911. Though unable to cry for help, the police dispatch was able to determine the origin of the call and send officers. When the units arrived, officers found Cheryl on the floor covered in the red fluid that not only gave, but saved, her life. Steve was still trying to accomplish his goal. The police subdued and arrested him. His clothes were completely soaked in Cheryl's blood.

Steve was convicted of domestic violence. He repeatedly called Cheryl from jail to tell her, "This is all your fault." He even threatened to kill himself.

Then, close to the day of sentencing, he wrote a note to Sheryl, removed the bed sheets, and hung himself in the small cell in which he was confined.

Steve's family, of course, blamed Cheryl. As she was not officially his wife, they took possession of the body, transported it to their home four states away, and never explained to Cheryl what had happened. That was my job now.

The emotional impact hit as hard and as ruthless as the beatings she had endured. Ever the victim, she finally said, "This is my fault. Had I just left rather than file charges he would still be alive."

It always infuriates me when the perpetrator continues to inflict pain even after they are gone. This was the only kind of "love" she had ever known. How would she ever be able to interpret God's love for her? God's love is unconditional and only holds us accountable for our own actions! Even then it is be filled with gentleness, kindness, understanding, and forgiveness.

I prayed earnestly that day for this lady. Oh, I set up the normal support systems. But Domestic Violence Intervention Services, Victim Counseling Services, and Family Survivors of Suicide could only give emotional coping skills. God alone could go deep into the soul and begin the healing of the giant crevasses that marred the spirit. Only God, by His Spirit, could help her begin to understand the difference between the love she had experienced and His love. That became the nature of our conversation that day. I could only pray that a miracle would take place. Not one of those walking-on-the-water miracles, just one of those where God's Holy Spirit finds a place to reside in the heart and begins to impart His faith, His wisdom, His love and His acceptance.

A week had passed. Now we stood in a parking lot next to where she worked. The people going in and out buying groceries had no idea what was transpiring just a few feet away. A woman, still in love with the man who tried to kill her and succeeded in taking his own life, was folding up his clothes -- clothes soaked in her blood. Stuffing the blood-filled clothes into a plastic bag, she tied it shut and tossed it into the back of my car. I closed the door.

"I've been thinking about what you said about God," she said. "I've asked Him to come into my life and teach me. He seems to be telling me this wasn't my fault. It was Steve's choice. Steve was the one who didn't know how to love. I am beginning to see my mistakes and yet feel God's acceptance. God has a better plan for me. With His help, I'm not going to settle for a victim's life ever again."

I prayed with her and drove away knowing she had found the answer. If she would hold onto that answer, trust God, and follow His directions about love, she would never have the same life again.

I smiled and called my wife, Susie, to tell her I was coming home.

Silver Bullet: Let no one degrade the wonderful soul within you. It was made in God's image and can be transformed into something of great value.

Shield: "I will praise thee; for I am fearfully and wonderfully made: marvelous are thy works; and that my soul knoweth right well." Psalm 139:14

Prayer: Lord, let not my failures nor anyone else's keep me from knowing how you have designed and are designing my life to have value and worth to You.

7

Our Best is Success

Wednesday, June 12, 7:30 a.m.

It was early in the morning when Patrice entered the local convenience store. Her blonde hair had been pulled into a ponytail. Her jogging suit was obviously a favorite as the Nike lettering had begun to fade from all the washing. Her brown eyes were surrounded by the right amount of eyeliner and makeup, yet her eyelids showed a slight droop from fatigue. Only those that knew her would have noticed. She had come in for her morning cup of cappuccino.

With a tired but cheery voice she said, "Good morning!" to the clerk behind the counter.

No one in the store except the clerk knew that Patrice was on the local paramedics. The ordinary looking citizen had spent the first part of the night cruising with her partner, Don, and answering the continuous calls for service that came over the radio. Each day they climbed into a large van-type vehicle, loaded with emergency equipment, and responded to one call after the other until the days' end.

On most days, many of the calls are surprisingly non-emergency in nature. A small child has her finger caught in the webbing of a lawn chair, one of the elderly citizens simply needs transport from the hospital to the nursing home, or someone's parrot has breathed its last, and the owner dials 911 for assistance. Like anything else in emergency service, nothing is as it appears on television. Last night, however, would etch itself in their memory for the rest of their life

As Patrice uttered her good morning to the clerk, he responded, "Well maybe for us, but did you hear about the policeman that was killed last night?"

"What!" exclaimed Patrice.

Pointing to the newspaper on the counter, he showed her the headlines that read in large bold type, "Police Officer Killed." With a shriek, Patrice grabbed the newspaper, fell against the wall, slid into the floor and began sobbing huge tears in the middle of the convenience store. No one understood. No one really could.

The previous evening, the police officer and his canine partner, Dino, had ventured into a dark alley after an armed suspect. It was a familiar routine. He would enter the alleyway, unleash the dog, and wait for the suspect to cry for help. Just as he was about to release his ever-faithful friend, a flash of light, a loud boom, and the smell of gunpowder filled the air. The call went out, "Shots fired! Officer down!"

Patrice and Don were the first to respond to the scene. This was the type of call they had prepared for all their life. This is the one that counts more than any other call in your career as a medic. When they arrived the scene was still "hot." The dog was attacking, the officer's partner has also been shot, and the gunfire continued. Two officers lay wounded and Patrice and her partner could not get in.

The minutes ticked by – like the grains of sand in the hour glass too large to slip through more than one at a time. Finally, they were given the "all clear" and were able to go in. The first officer was seriously wounded. They focused their attention on him and gave it everything they had. After stabilization and transport, they sat in the E.R. together with solemn faces awaiting the outcome. Had they done enough? Were they soon enough? They couldn't leave until they knew.

At approximately 1:30 a.m., the answer came. The prognosis looked good. He was stable and with any luck at all, would pull through. Too fatigued and grateful to show much excitement, they gathered their equipment and prepared to end their shift. Sleep would be good tonight.

Somewhere during the night the prognosis changed. Things went from bad to worse and within a few hours of Patrice and Don leaving, the officer took his last breath and went on to face his Maker. Patrice and Don would be asleep. Patrice wouldn't find out until that morning she stepped into the convenience store and the clerk pointed to the early edition.

Now they were both in my office. Don sat with his elbows on his knees and his face in his hands. Patrice had leaned all the way back against the wall, hands in her lap. and had slid herself forward on the seat. The two of them sat side by side staring into the carpet. Their white shirts were ironed and starched to a razor sharp edge. Their shoes were not the type that would polish to a high sheen but looked very comfortable.

Both of them looked up at me with tear-reddened eyes. "I feel so helpless. I don't know how we can face the other officers tonight. I prayed so hard for this guy. I just knew he was going to make it. I went home feeling so good. I can't believe I fell apart so quickly in a convenience store. I thought I could handle this job. Now I don't know if I can."

I didn't know if she could handle it anymore either. All of us hurt. It was the classic case of the wounded trying to lead the wounded to healing. Three wounded people attempting to cope with a difficult reality. None of us get to decide who lives or who dies. We could only decide if we cared enough to give our best. That is all. It seems so little until you compare it to so many of the world. Those who live their lives for the betterment of themselves never experience the grandeur of putting themselves on the line for another. I don't mean just your life, but some of the very things that make up life. Things like temporary happiness, feelings of security, faith that nothing bad can happen, and those precious feelings that everything is in control. Every police officer, firefighter, and paramedic puts that kind of life on the line every day. To give up even one of those things can be as hard as dying itself.

Yet everyday they get up and do it again. Finding a faith that was challenged the day before and using it to face the coming one.

<center>~~~</center>

Silver Bullet: Doing right is no guarantee against misfortune. It can, however, guarantee the satisfaction of having done the best you could.

Shield: "He who follows righteousness and mercy finds life, righteousness and honor." Proverbs 21:21 (NKJV)

Prayer: Lord, when I have done my best, put my skill to the test, yet failed at success, help me place the result in Your hands and rise to love again.

8

Defining Moments

Thursday, March 21, 11:30 a.m.

Isn't it strange how time, though measured in specific and standard increments, can be described by such varying degrees of speed? We make appointments using time as a key tool for finding someone else. By the use of time, we can meet a stranger at a certain location in another part of the world based simply on a clock.

Yet time can drag. It can run out or go on forever. We can do a lot of things if someone will "just give me a minute." It can be quick as a flash.... or slow as molasses.... all depending on what is taking place during a certain increment of time. A boring book can make an hour seem like a day. Yet an interesting one filled with things that stir the imagination may make the same hour feel much shorter. Regardless, time is a precious commodity afforded simply based by the grace of God. John Thomas was to learn the importance of time. A car crash and a fire would help.

The top of John's head was probably six feet and four inches from the sole of his feet. He was a hard-working good old boy in his late twenties. From his wide shoulders his body tapered to a thirty-two inch waist. Dressed in a red flannel shirt, Levi blue jeans, work boots, the entire ensemble accented with a leather belt and an oval shaped silver buckle, he was the picture of an Oklahoma cowboy. It's hard to tell what a hero looks like. Today one would look like John Thomas.

With the window of his truck rolled all the way down and the western wind blowing hot across his face, he hardly noticed how tanned his arm had become as it rested on the windowsill of the shiny pickup. Only the best could tell his beautiful blue machine wasn't new. As he rounded one of the long curves of the expressway, a blue Chevy El Camino came into view. It sat halfway on the shoulder of the road, upside down, fuel dripping from the gas tank, and fire lapping around the hood into the cab of the vehicle. As traffic began to slow, John eased onto the shoulder and drove up to the overturned burning vehicle.

A woman with scared eyes and burns visible on her face and arms approached him screaming, "My mother is still in there!"

Inside the burning half-car half-truck sat a small statured seventy-four year old, unable to free herself from the wreckage. The flames were now burning larger, higher, and billowing black smoke into the air. As the little woman sat helpless, a pair of huge arms reached through the flames and pulled her from the burning wreckage. Shortly after, the fuel tank exploded. The ambulance arrived and transported them all to the burn center, including John.

The community would soon come to know of John's heroic effort. Two weeks later, a special luncheon was held in his honor. His family had come to watch the young man receive the "Good Samaritan" award. His face and arms were cherry red and covered with a salve of some sort, giving his face the appearance of a shiny apple. His hands were covered in a cloth wrapping that showed yellowed patches where burn medicine had seeped through the cloth. His boots thumped the floor as he took long lanky strides to the podium to receive the honor. Cameras whirred and flashed as he turned to face the audience. Many of them were family members of the lady he pulled from the fiery crash.

He spoke in a broken voice, words of people's commitment to each other, the preciousness of life, and how he wished that little old lady could have lived more than just a few days after his efforts. To him, her death seemed to cheapen his attempt. After all, he was trying to save a life. Describing his desire, he broke down into tears. We were all very moved.

At the end of his acceptance speech, his long cowboy legs took him back to his table. A few final remarks from the master of ceremonies and all were dismissed. One of the victim's daughters came to place a hug around John. His burns only allowed her to place her head on his chest, squeeze his waist, and say, "Thank you. You are a wonderful man."

With his head down John simply said, "No ma'am. I shoulda been there sooner. I sure wanted to give you your mom back."

Oh, Mr. Thomas," she said. "Because of you we were able to tell her how much we loved her before she left us. Because of you, grandchildren who had not seen her in years were able to be by her side. Because of you, a son she had not seen in years was able to make amends with his mother and brothers and sisters. You gave us what we didn't know we had and could have lost. Mr. Thomas, you gave us time -- and we will be forever grateful."

~⌣ ⌣⌣

Silver Bullet: Time can be filled or emptied with many things of our choosing . . . a loud voice raised in anger or a soft one filled with compassion. Use it to take an "eye for an eye" and everyone will be blind -- or use it to see what can be made better and bring light to everyone.

Shield: "Whereas you do not know what will happen tomorrow. For what is your life? It is even a vapor that appears for a little time and then vanishes away." James 4:14

Prayer: Oh Lord, give me strength in a time of weakness, power in a time of adversity, and help me to fill my days with Your good.

9

Seventy Times Seven

Friday, January 5, 08:15 .am.

The old man looked a bit lost wandering the hallway of the police department. It was obvious he was not accustomed to such surroundings. His eyes dimmed by the years, he had to step close to the many signs before he could read the titles and directions displayed there for the public. You and I have seen his old coat on a hundred different people. Yet, the worn green reversible coat with the hunter orange collar and liner somehow picked up an air of dignity from its wearer.

I was close behind one of our officers when he asked the old man if he needed help finding his way around. "I've come to bail out my son", the old man said with a wrinkled smile and gleaming eyes. It was a look that seemed proud of his actions but embarrassed that he had to be there. It seemed so strange that one look could say so much.

The big cop boomed, "Who is your son?" When the old man told him, the policeman shook his head and said, "Bet you have had to do this several times! I don't know that I would waste my time and money."

The old man responded with, "I suppose you are right, but he is my son. I put a lot of time into raising him right. He got in with the wrong crowd. He knows what is right and wrong and soon enough he'll come around."

I stood there like a third arm with nothing to do, yet fascinated by this conversational exchange. The officer continued, "I have arrested him twice myself. Some people are just no good from the git-go and you don't need to be wasting your money and worry on this kid." The officer wasn't trying to be cruel. He genuinely felt for the old man.

I watched the embarrassed old man drop his eyes as if he really had nothing else he could say and we got on the elevator together. He was a bit stooped over and had to look up to see into anyone else's face. I smiled as he looked at me with a very concerned countenance and said, "Well, a man has to believe in his son, I guess."

He stepped off the elevator and up to the plate glass window, looked up at the receptionist with his gray eyes once again twinkling with friendliness and warmth. He smiled at the lady, took out a handful of wrinkled money, and in a cheery voice said, "I'm here to bail out my son!"

I left wondering how many times God bails out his children and just how much is seventy times seven?

~⌣⌣∿

Silver Bullet: Sometimes it is hard to believe how many chances God is willing to give us. Yet, over and over again He invests in us. That is what love does.

Shield: " If ye then, being evil, know how to give good gifts unto your children, how much more shall your Father which is in heaven give good things to them that ask him?"
Matthew. 7:11

Prayer: Lord, help me not give up on me. Help me to think like You. Help me to act like You. Help me to believe about me as You do.

10

Character + Commitment = Confidence

Friday, June 19, 10:45 p.m.

The way the night had been going, I never thought of wanting a big cop around. Yet everything escalated so quickly that we were in trouble before I had time to anticipate and fear. All evening it had been one boring call after another. I soon observed that policeman are often to society what a teacher is to kindergarten. Not very much is really taught, but you have to keep all the kids in line and listen to their whining. "He parked his car too close to my driveway. Make him move it." "They are always complaining about my radio being too loud, make them turn their lights off at a decent hour." "His dog came over and crapped in my yard. I want him to clean it up!" It really gets old sometimes.

That was the type of night it had been. When the call "man waving a gun" came across the radio, almost everyone assumed the police would show up, the man with the gun would be long gone, and we would check back in for the next teacher's assignment.

The complex was known for street gangs and anti-cop sentiments. An officer hardly ever went there alone. Our patrol car came up one end of the street. Another came the other way. We met in the middle. Standing in front of us were three men. One of whom matched the description of the one waving a gun. As the cruiser pulled up, the three men separated and began walking away. Each of them ignored the officers as they demanded that the men talk to them. One young man walked past our car. The officer I was with asked him to stop. The officer was ignored. The man kept walking. This time the officer demanded that he stop. He refused. With one deft move, the officer grabbed the man by the neck and had him face down on the trunk of the unit.

In a flash, angry people came from everywhere! Yelling at us, pushing, trying to get to the officer. It was downright scary! We were vastly outnumbered and the crowd was getting in a feverish pitch. From the back of the squad car, in a flash of green, came the smallest cop I had ever seen. She appeared to be barely over five feet tall and could not have weighed 100 lbs. With authoritative sincerity, she waded into the crowd with her nightstick held horizontally across her chest, pushed back a group of the angry mob and demanded that they calm down and talk this out.

I had met Officer Karen Rovan earlier at the squad meeting and remember thinking, if we get in trouble, what is **she** going to do? We all like to think we have conquered our prejudices, but in reality we struggle with them most of our lives. Few people know what it is like to be a female in law enforcement. Karen faced more than being a female. She was a lightweight, she was short, and she didn't play the politics that women sometimes have to play to get anywhere in law enforcement. She just did her job. . . . with fairness, tenacity, and intelligence.

That was seventeen years ago. I thought then, she is brave, she is good, but she will never get ahead in this occupation. This morning as I walked down the hallway at the downtown headquarters, there was a lot of the "brass" coming in for Monday morning staff meeting.

The words, "Morning, Chaplain" came from behind me.

I turned and said, "Well, Morning, CAPTAIN Rovan!"

Silver Bullet: The limitations you accept are the only ones that will guide your life.

Shield: "I can do all things through Christ who strengthens me." Philippians 4: 13

Prayer: Lord, Help me not to place limitations on myself nor let my prejudices allow me to place them on others. For all people can do great things who put their faith in God.

11

A Four Year Old's Guilt

Wednesday, August 12, 09:30 a.m.

Anyone who has been in law enforcement very long can remember some particular civilian or officer-motivated program that resulted in the requirement for one or more objects to be placed in the squad car. It could have been as small as a business card with referrals for domestic violence treatment, or as large as a teddy bear. I liked the teddy bears. It was a memorable day when they issued the chaplain's department teddy bears. It meant we were part of the team. That wonderful team called law enforcement. Somehow, it was one of those "rights of passage" that come unexpectedly, yet mark our lives just the same.

My teddy bear always worked. I have given them to crying children more than once and watched as their new friend gave them the comfort and warmth they needed at the time. I once sat in the back yard with two small girls whose sister had just drowned in the neighbor's swimming pool and, upon receiving their furry fake pet, quieted down and began to care for their new companion.

Tommy was my one exception. It was strange to be called to a house fire in the summertime. One of the things that winter usually brings is fire fatalities. The old heaters are lit, fireplaces stoked, people closed inside for longer periods of time, all of these things are conducive to fires. But summertime is different.

This house burned so quickly. It started in a back bedroom. . . the baby's room. Officer's had blocked off traffic. The bright red fire trucks were filling the air with the smell of diesel fuel as the engines idled. It always amazes me how much water leaks around a fire truck. Water was everywhere. Smoke and steam rose very slowly from the little home. Everyone was curious as to how the fire started. Tommy's eight-month-old sister did not escape the blaze. Fire fighters found her still in her crib. Tommy was four.

When I arrived, Tommy and his mother were in the back seat of the Fire Department station wagon. Mom was wearing the shock mask. The one that has a thousand pondering thoughts without one answer. Tommy was crying so loudly that no one could talk. His blonde hair, cut in a long flat top style that had long outgrown itself, was almost brown where the ends were soaked with sweat. His face was so fair that the smut and dirt showed up easily across his flushed cheeks. Tears cut little furrows along the fertile soil on his young face. He sat in his mother's lap, facing away from her, with his fists clenched and crying loudly. So loud that no one could talk to mom to comfort her.

Remembering the "magic" cure, I walked back to my car, opened the back door, and grabbed "Teddy." Walking triumphantly back to the station wagon, I handed Tommy the friendly stuffed animal. Those piercing blue, tear-filled eyes stared at me as though he knew about our adult ploy. He never reached for the stuffed toy at all. Just looked at me crying as if to say, do you really think <u>that</u> can help me? The eyes of a four year old had made me feel guilty. As if he knew I was making too light of a deal here. The offer had absolutely no affect at all. It had always worked. I put the bear back in the car and once again approached the station wagon.

As I sat across the seat watching this heart-broken young boy cry, I noticed both hands were still in a clenched fist but his right thumb was making a familiar motion. Over and over again his thumb would go up and down. He kept staring at it. So much so that I thought he had been burned there. I took him into my arms and walked him around by the big fire truck. Fire trucks always fascinated kids. He just buried his head in my shoulder and kept his little fist clenched, moving his thumb up and down. I took his hand and looked to see if it were burned. It was not. Suddenly the motion he was making made sense to me. It was just like the motion you make when striking a cigarette lighter. "Tommy, does your hand hurt?"

Those teary little eyes stared at me as if trying to get a message, and through convulsing stomach muscles Tommy said, "I did it."

Silver Bullet: Unlike children, we often feel we can make our guilt go away by covering our pain with things we love. Yet, sometimes its best to look into the eyes of God and say, "I did it." There we will find the forgiveness, the acceptance, and the love that can place the healing balm on the wounds of our transgression.

Shield: "For if we confess our sin, He is faithful and just to forgive us our sin and cleanse us from all unrighteousness." 1 John 1:9

Prayer: Lord, I have tried to cover my pain in so many ways and nothing seems to work. So now I bring my pain and my sin to You to ask for Your forgiveness and healing that comes from the death of Christ my Savior.

12

The Love of Liota

Monday, September 9, 10:30 a.m.

Liota lived in a small wood frame house with white-shingled siding. The kind built as a tract house in the 1950's. You know the look, white shingles, black shutters, black roof, small yard with a birdbath. The 50's were good years. They were the years after World War II when the economy really began to blossom and bring an automobile and a modest home to blue collar America. Liota's home was a picture of the 50's, with one very small garage, two very small bedrooms, and one very small bathroom equipped with simply what was necessary. A small sink, a small bathtub, a small mirror, a small everything. I guess people didn't spend as much time in the bathroom in the 50's as they do now. Or at least the activities didn't vary as much.

For 48 years Liota had lived there. The last fifteen or so, all alone. Her youthful appearance had long left. Her hairstyle looked like one out of the 1950's, except it was done in gray with bluish hues and well groomed. Her face and body had gotten a lot more round. Her eyes had a lot more crow's feet, but her smile still looked adolescent. Her small car, like herself, was not in the best of health, but if you babied it, it would eventually accomplish the task. People who lived around her never heard much from her and probably assumed she didn't do much more than watch the soap operas parade across her small TV screen.

There is a special room in hospitals where families are taken to be given terrible news. I hate that room. Yet, I found myself thanking God that it was available. It was late afternoon and I was on my way to that room to meet another family. A group of children had been swimming in a neighbor's pool. The loud shrieks and laughing could be heard for blocks as the children played and splashed in the cool water under the hot sun. Seven-year-old Latisha drowned that afternoon in full view of all her sisters and friends. They wanted to save her. None of them knew how.

Parents and siblings waited on me in that quiet room. They knew in their heart what I was about to tell them. They just hadn't been able to get their mind to accept the news. I told them as lovingly as I could. The grief was as you would imagine. Latisha's two-and-a-half year old sister began to cry. Those big eyes looking around the room for some sort of comfort. You could see the fear. She was too young to know about death, but was quite cognizant that mom and dad were very upset. Her protection and safety system seemed to be out of control and she cried for fear and confusion more than anything else. You may find words to bring some comfort to an adult, but a child this young left me feeling incredibly helpless.

Taking her into my arms, I walked her and her older sister outside to my car. Opening the trunk revealed a bag full of brand new stuffed animals. Holding the little girl toward the open bag, she was told to pick out any toy she wanted. It would be hers. Just hers. With eyes still moist, looking with disbelief, she sorted through the bag until stumbling across Woody Woodpecker. Grabbing his bright blue body with brilliant red head and yellow beak, she held it close to her body and smiled. A smile in the midst of such tragedy is priceless!!!

The little girl calmed down and went back into that room confident and more secure. She held up her new prize to show her mom. Mom and Dad had now composed themselves and perhaps everything was going to be all right. The family and others thought I was wonderful having worked such magic. They didn't know the real miracle worker was a little old lady who lived in a small 50's tract house and collected new stuffed toys to be given freely to children in trouble.

And just so you don't forget, her name is Liota.

~

Silver Bullet: The greatness of a community is not always defined by the grandeur of its buildings, the wealth of its economy, or extent of its opportunities for advancement. Sometimes greatness is little old ladies that give Woody Woodpeckers to children.

Shield: "And those members of the body, which we think to be less honorable, upon these we bestow more abundant honor." I Corinthians 12:23

Prayer: Lord, help me realize that everything I do for You and for others is special to You.

13

The Ministry of Violence

Thursday, October 3, 3:00 p.m.

There are a lot of wonderful words of wisdom that can be heard from the front seat of a squad car. Wisdom sometimes passed down from older cops or just learned as the beat goes on. Some of it beneficial, some of it of no real use but to bring about the knowing smile or laughter that can only come after years of doing the job.

Here are some of them: "The handcuffs are tight because they are new. They'll stretch out after you wear them awhile." Or "No sir, we don't have quotas anymore. We used to have quotas but now we can write as many as we want!" Or even, "Life's tough, it's tougher if you're stupid."

I guess there is one in particular that caused me a great deal of thought. In its attempt to be funny, there is more truth in it than I may find comfortable. It goes to the very core of Christian commitment for a police officer, wrestles with his conscious, and calls into conflict his ideal of Christianity and the practical living of it in a uniform. It goes something like this... "Law abiding citizens sleep peacefully in their beds, solely because dedicated men and women stand ready to do violence in their behalf."

It is somewhat like giving the name "Peace Keeper Missile" to a nuclear warhead. When actually its sole authority lies within both its ability and reliability to perform an act that is not peaceful at all. Sooner or later, a police officer will serve as a peacekeeper by resorting to violence. Oh for the day that it will not be necessary!!! But, today it is! Until the spirit of Christ comes to lock the evil away, there will still be a call for the David's to stand up to the Goliaths, the Deborah's to conquer evil kings, and our mighty men and women of valor to stand and be counted among the valiant.

The book of Revelation describes the return of the Holy Spirit. He will come victorious, surrounded by the host of heaven arrayed in battle gear. His eyes will be as a flame of fire, His words as a sharpened sword. Power and authority will be His strength, retribution His reward, and justice His goal. Somehow, I can't help but believe there will be a police officer in the host.

I can hear the seasoned veteran of law enforcement remark to the evil one, "If you run, you'll just go to jail tired!"

Silver Bullet: The fact that you are compelled to use force does not make you a person of violence. Only the one who seeks violence as a way of personal gain or an avenue for quick solution is determined to be violent.

Shield: "For he is the minister of God to thee for good. But if thou do that which is evil, be afraid; for he beareth not the sword in vain: for he is the minister of God, a revenger to execute wrath upon him that doeth evil." Romans 13:4

Prayer: Lord, keep my feet from following violence. Yet, should it cross my path, let me be strong in the power of your might.

14

Correction and Perfection

Monday, May 6, 2:00 p.m.

The engine of the small Cessna 150 purred with precision as Susie and I continued on our journey toward Memphis. We had left Tulsa early that morning under clear skies. A front had passed through a day or so before and was still in Memphis but was scheduled to pass before we would get there. As every pilot knows, the weather sometimes refuses to cooperate. A little over halfway there, we caught up with it. Rain mixed with low clouds forced us to set down in Russellville, Arkansas.

Nothing to do now but wait. After a few hours we tried it again. Again our efforts were thwarted by a slow moving front and down we went again. Another two hours and up we went, and down we came. A simple three-and-a -half hour trip was now seven hours in the making.

I was new to piloting. This was my first cross county trip after receiving my private pilot's license. Now I had a decision to make. Darkness was not far away. We were only sixty miles from the small airport but the front was just passing by. I made a phone call to my brother in Memphis, hoping he could give me advice. When I got him on the phone, he described the conditions as best he could. I asked him, "Do you think I can make it?"

His response taught me a great lesson about life. "Danny, it looks like one of those gray winter days."

I pondered what that could mean and asked, "Yes, but can I make it?"

His reply, "I don't know, man, you the pilot!"

I'm the pilot! I wanted someone else to be responsible for my decision. I wanted someone else to tell me what to do. But he was right. I was the pilot! A long pause preceded my next statement. "I'm coming!" I told him. "Meet me at the airport. We will be there in thirty minutes!"

We crawled back in the little two-seated airplane, pointed it down the runway, pushed full throttle, and turned the nose upward. We were off into clear skies. Climbing to 4500 feet I could see the line of clouds in front of us. Soon, sparse clouds gathered beneath us and then we were on top of a world of snowy white. It was beautiful from that position. Below us the clouds formed pillowy pictures of every creature imaginable. The shadow of the little Cessna could be easily seen just beneath us. As if to show how special we were, our shadow was encircled by a tiny rainbow. It was absolutely breathtaking. Clear blue sky around us, cottony softness below us. A world I had never seen before.

It was then I realized that I could not see the airport, the ground, or anything in between. I didn't know how close the clouds were to the ground or if there were tall buildings, obstructions, or towers around the airport. I was going to have to find the airport in the blind. The desire to just get there never allowed me to think of turning back. It was dumb. Pride can make a man very, very stupid.

I took out a map of the terrain and it showed no towers or buildings. Turning to the weather report station for Memphis International, I learned that the ceiling was 900 feet. The airport was 230 feet above sea level. That left me 630 feet of clear sky between the clouds and the ground. All I had to do now was get through the clouds at the right place and I should be able to see the airfield. To do that, I would have to completely trust the instruments. I had only done that with a certified flight instructor next to me. Flying in the clouds is extremely dangerous. If you trust your feelings and fly by the seat of your pants, it is deadly!

My GPS (Global Positioning System) told me the airport was ten miles away. I set the throttle for a standard rate of descent. I decided I would keep the wings level, stay on course for the airport, and watch the altimeter. If I didn't see the ground by 800 feet, I would turn the nose up, get on top of the clouds again, and fly back toward home.

At 3300 feet, Susan and I dropped into the clouds. It was the scariest time I can remember. Susan prayed and I watched the instruments. Standard rate of descent, wings level, heading true, so far so good. My mind told me I was making a left turn in the cloudbank. The instruments said I was flying straight. I fought off my feelings and forced myself to trust the instruments.

Twenty-five hundred feet, two thousand, fifteen hundred, we were approaching the decision altitude and no land in sight.

One thousand, nine hundred, eight fifty, eight hundred, and still no land. As I started to put pressure on the yoke to pull the plane upward, there was a break in the clouds and I could see pay dirt! Down another fifty feet and we were under the clouds. There was the airport!!! Right where it was supposed to be!!! After circling the airfield, we landed smoothly at Hernando Village airport. I taxied across the turf field, pulled the fuel mixture, and starved the engine to a stop.

I had learned that I was the pilot. That many circumstances we face are a result of our own decisions. I can't hold anyone else responsible. I alone could be held accountable for the decisions I make in life.

I also learned that the instruments and map were invaluable tools after having made a dumb decision. Life is like that. Your Bible is the road map to life. It tells you where the obstacles are. Sometimes everything may be telling you to go in one direction, but your Bible will always be right. Even after bad decisions, it will lead you safely home. You can trust God's word.

Silver Bullet: Decisions may not be reversible, but they are always fixable in God's world.

Shield: "Trust in the Lord with all thine heart; and lean not unto thine own understanding. In all thy ways acknowledge him, and he shall direct thy paths." Proverbs 3:5,6

Prayer: Father, let me not be wise in my own eyes, but learn to be led of You day by day.

15

Our Voice Heard by One

Monday, March 1.15, 9:30 a.m.

Each of us has those moments in life when we desperately want to say the right thing or do the right thing for someone who is hurting. Yet there seem to be no words or way we can do much of anything but be present. During those times, there is a conversation being carried on that no one but the hurting may hear, even above their grief.

I shall never forget Terrel McPeoples. Only two months old. yet he left such a powerful impression on my life. He and his single mother lived in an apartment in the low-income side of Tulsa. Every town has a low-income side. Tulsa is not unlike a lot of cities. Remarkably beautiful for the most part, but has its places where no one can afford to do much fixing up. Terrel was born in such a place. He died there, in the middle of the night, for no apparent reason, only two months old. SIDS. Sudden Infant Death Syndrome. The cause that explains a new life just leaving here and going to be with the Lord.

The apartment was dimly lit. The carpet was out-of-date green shag. There was one telephone that used to be white with a long cord that allowed you to take it into any room of the small single-family dwelling. Terrel's young mother was seated on the old couch with her mother and sobbing convulsively. It was easy to see that Terrel was all she had. Rejected by her husband. No chance for a real education. No money to buy anything more than just what helped you get by. This child had brought joy and meaning into her life. She went to bed that night enamored with a young life that could receive all the love she could give -- and woke up to find it gone.

There wasn't much of a church history for me to call upon. She was so grief stricken there were no words a mortal could say to bring her comfort. I wanted to tell her all the spiritual things. "He is with the Lord. He is in a better place." All those things are true, but at the time seemed to give little comfort. I felt so helpless. The medical examiner arrived to investigate the scene and take the little body away. I thought, if I were this mom, I would want to hold this baby one more time. To some it may sound morbid, but not to those who have been there.

"Ms. McPeoples, would you like to hold Terrel before they take him?" I asked.

With eyes that looked filled with anticipation at the possibility, she spoke quietly, "Could I please?"

I led her into the tiny bedroom and sat her in a chair. On the bed was tiny Terrel. He looked asleep. His little pudgy fingers looked so incredibly tiny! His little round face and dark eyebrows had an almost angelic appearance. I wrapped the little guy in a blanket and tenderly handed him to his mother. She took him into her arms and released a loud shriek followed by wave after wave of heart wrenching sobs. Her mother came into the room. Neither of us could console her.

Finally, it seemed as if the Lord said to each of us, "just leave her alone." As grandmother and I talked to each other over her shrieks of grief, we both prayed.

Suddenly the room was quiet except for Terrel's mother singing in a soft and broken voice. A song that I had heard from my youngest days in church now, for the first time, had the meaning for which it was intended.

Grandmother and I listened reverently as Terrel was being held by his mother singing…."Jesus…loves me……this I know. For the

Bible......tells...me... so. LITTLE ONES TO HIM BELONG.......
THEY ARE WEAK BUT HE IS STRONG!"

I was dumb struck! What we couldn't do, God had done by simply recalling in her memory a song she heard as a child. Through it, He had let her know the assurance and peace of His care.

The medical examiner took Terrel with him. Everyone that arrived, the firefighters, the police officers, family, everyone was filled with compassion and care. Floral Haven funeral home even provided the funeral service free of charge.

No one, however, had more affect than a simple song breathed across her heart by the breath of God. "Jesus loves me this I know............"

<hr>

Silver Bullet: You and I are not called upon to do it all. Just what we can. Trust that God is there to do His part.

Shield: " . . . not by might, nor by power, but my spirit, says the Lord of Hosts."
Zechariah 4: 6 (NKJ)

Prayer: Lord, give me the confidence that where I am weak, you can be strong.

16

Don't Fly Against the Numbers

Saturday, August 1, 1:00 p.m.

Flying back from Memphis in our single engine Piper Tri Pacer had been a wonderful experience. Although it was not Instrument Flight Rated, I had installed, not one, but two GPS systems for navigation. I love that airplane. Its rich, dark green paint job accented by gold and maroon stripes made it an eye catcher at many of the airports. Often called "the flying milk stool" because of its tricycle landing gear, it had set the standard in the early days. It was referred to as the business and family airplane. 1950's advertising prophesied that there would be one in every garage in America. Trustworthy, solid, fuel efficient, these were words that described it. I had other words. Words like, beautiful, peaceful, thrilling, could only begin to describe how I felt when piloting the little plane.

The GPS was the most up to date means of piloting I could find. It could locate your position anywhere in the world, accept the name of your destination airport, and calculate the distance, direction, and time of travel within a few meters and seconds. While you were in the air, it would adjust your direction if you varied off course, calculate your ground speed at any given time, constantly update your time of arrival, and alert you to any controlled airspace you may be approaching. In the event of trouble in the air, a push of a button calculated the closest airports and within seconds, give you the directions and distance to it . . . a phenomenal piece of navigation equipment.

A man-made satellite placed in the heavens transmitted a man-made signal to a man-made receiver and made all flight calculations on a man-made computer. I had depended on it faithfully. Even when I found myself surrounded by clouds and unable to see land, it guided me directly to the hidden airport. I loved it. With the backup GPS system, I made the mistake of solely depending on it for navigation.

Coming back from Memphis I had programmed in the appropriate airports, set the nose of the Piper in the right direction, and headed into the wild blue beautiful yonder. Somewhere over Conway, Arkansas, the GPS mounted on the yoke of my airplane said, "Satellite Connection Lost". That means any direction it gives you is inaccurate. For some reason, it was no longer tracking. The antennae could have been bad. A power drop may have caused it. But, no worry, I thought. I have the backup GPS. Taking it from my flight bag, I plugged it in, placed its antennae in the windshield and turned it on. Another reality came home. I had not used the GPS in months and the unit needed to be reset. That would take forty-five minutes or more. I flew my last known course, picking out landmarks in between dinking with the secondary GPS.

I realized the problem was a power problem. The GPS kept trying to reset itself. Two units and I could not depend on either one! Go figure!! I had the VOR radios (pilot talk for high frequency navigational radio), but repeated trips across this same area had lulled me into not writing down those frequencies for the VOR stations needed. These man-made objects, in spite of their sophistication, had let me down. There was one thing that didn't. . . .the simple magnetic compass on the dash of the airplane. It gave me an accurate direction and by simply watching my landmarks, I could fly to my destination. The compass didn't rely on man-made signals. It was working by a force that God had put into place when he created the earth...... **Magnetism!!! It was**

always there!! It never malfunctioned! God had made it...not man. I could count on it!!

—

Silver Bullet: Because man is imperfect, whatever he creates is marked by his imperfection. Whatever God creates, is marked by His trustworthiness.

Shield: "It is better to trust in the Lord, than to put confidence in man." Psalms 118:8

Prayer: Lord, help me not be surprised at the inadequacies of man nor forget Your faithfulness, for I can trust You.

17

Silk Purse from a Sow's Ear

Tuesday, May 27, 11:00 a.m.

Police work can bring to view some of the greatest acts of benevolence from some of the most unlikely people under the strangest of circumstances. The ability to observe these is only a pleasure and privilege to those who recognize them. These incredible acts of simple kindness may be missed by the officer who envisions his occupation as separate from his or her personal life. It is far better, I think, to believe God has something special in each call. . . something personal.

Officer Bailey was assigned a call on Admiral Court. It was pretty cut and dried. A seventy-three year old white male had run out of reasons for getting up in the morning. Not only had living alone become hard on him, but just living at all had become unbearable. The house and all the furnishings were much like him. They were not in bad shape. They were just old. It is strange how a house can become a reflection of its owner. Everything in it seemed to reflect his age and generation. He had shelves and shelves of books…. old ones. Each room was filled with precious possessions of yesteryear.

There were paintings of all sizes with no sense of continuity to them, as if each of them represented a different stage in his life. There were small ivory carvings placed in strategic places throughout the residence. His wife had passed away some time before, but he left "Martha's" room just as she had left it. He slept in another room. That is where he was found. And not by family, for he had outlived most of them, but interestingly enough, by the used car salesman that came over that morning to close the deal on a second-hand Buick. He found the patron stretched out on his bed atop a 1940's quilt. A 9mm semi automatic with one round fired lay on the old man's chest. A note giving directions on how to handle the remains lay nearby.

The front window had been broken out. Just two nights before, he had locked himself out of the house. In a drunken rage, he threw a large brick through the window.

I pulled up to the house two days after the body had been found. We were not able to locate any family. I was going inside to check through some of his old mail and address books to see if there was any hint of a distant relative of some kind. It appeared as if this was one life that didn't matter much. I am embarrassed to say that I even began to believe it myself.

Across the street from the residence in this old run down neighborhood, a very round, rough, burley looking man watched as I pulled up. His dark hair was long and unkept. It was matted from perspiration. A long full beard covered his face and seemed to grow into his unkept hair. His huge stomach bulged out from under his too small tee shirt, the front of which was filthy from where his protruding appendage had rubbed whatever objects he had been carrying. I really don't know if it was dirt or hours in the sun that gave him his brown skin. My hand gave a slight wave just to let him know he had been observed and I was not intimidated by his presence. That was probably a half-truth.

Walking upon the porch, I observed the most beautiful bouquet of flowers I had ever seen. It literally painted the porch with colors of purple, red, yellow, and white. It, along with a sympathy card, had been placed on a small end table in front of the entrance. I opened the card to read, "He was our friend. Please accept our condolences in your time of sorrow." It was signed by more than twenty people!

The old man across the street walked up on me almost unnoticed. In a loud, yet raspy, voice he said, "You with the police?"

"Yes, yes I am. Do you know where these flowers came from?"

What few teeth he had gleamed through his full black beard as he said, "Yessir, I growed 'em. Lot's of us neighbors knew him. He may have had a bit of a drinkin' problem but he was awful good to us. None of us knowed his family and we didn't have no money for flowers. But…I kinda always had a gift for growin' thangs. So I pulled these out of my garden, went down and bought this card, and it seemed like people liked it. Lots of 'em came by and signed it."

Just a few minutes ago I was making judgments on the value of such a neighbor. Now I hope to have one as thoughtful and sincere when I leave this earth. Taking my radio in my hand, I called out the designator of the officer that initially worked the scene. I showed him the flowers and introduced him to the old boy that "growed 'em." It seemed the right thing to do. The officer seemed appreciative.

I eventually found family. They lived in Texas. They came up and disposed of all the paintings and books, sold the house and went back to Texas. There was no funeral, not even a graveside service. In fact, the only flowers marking the passing on of a human being were those left by a rough, round, rustic, roustabout who had " a gift for growin' thangs."

A simple gift, yet it gave an avenue of expression for those that loved -- and a certain dignity to the death of a neighbor. What small gift do you have?

〜〜〜

Silver Bullet: We cannot all do great things, but we can do small things with great love.

-Mother Theresa

Shield: "Now he who plants and he who waters are one, and each one will receive his own reward according to his own labor." I Cor.3: 8 (NKJV)

Prayer: Lord, help me realize that what I do for you has great significance. When done out of true compassion, it is rewarded in heavenly earnings and is of no small value to you.

18

So You Want to be Rich?

Tuesday, September 17, 9:00 a.m.

She stood in the middle of her front yard with both hands up in the air as high as she could reach. Her head was tilted back and the locks of her African American hair fell straight down her back. Tears streamed down her face as she said aloud, over and over again, "Thank you, Jesus. Thank you, Jesus."

The neighbors began to stare out their doors, not daring to come over. The street in front of the house became a parking lot for a fire truck, an ambulance, and two police cars.

Admittedly, a strange place to hold a worship service, but the middle-aged lady kept right on worshipping God, unaware of who came and went. "Thank you, Jesus. Thank you, Jesus. Oh...I worship you, Lord. Blessed be Your name, O God. You are mighty and strong. Full of love and mercy." On and on and on she went. Not appearing to be mental, just lost in sincere worship.

Officer John Beaver met me in the front yard. He pulled me to the side and said, "Chaplain, an elderly gentleman has passed away. He was 82. His wife is in the living room. This is one of his daughters here in the front yard. Chaplain," he said, "now be careful where you sit in there. The house is crawling with bugs."

The signs of poverty were everywhere. The dimly lit rooms illuminated by a single light bulb in an inexpensive socket. No chandeliers here. No swinging lamps. Just what was necessary. The wooden floor had long ago lost its sheen. Some of the boards were actually worn through. Mamma, in her long cotton dress, sat in the rocker trying to grasp the fact that sixty years of marriage had come to an end. The house was full of children and grandchildren all expressing their grief in one manner or another. The old man's heart had just stopped beating. He was gone.

Just a few weeks ago, I approached a home whose owner had experienced the same demise. Yet the contrast was startling. The home was huge, 5000 square feet or more. It was filled with polished wood floors, plush carpet, statues collected from all over the world, gigantic chandeliers, a private library, and a three-car garage filled with expensive modes of transportation. He died in his bedroom too. The coroner said, " an apparent heart attack." He wasn't found by family. As the maid reported for work that day, she was unable to raise a response from his bedroom. She opened the door and found him on the floor in a fetal position. He died alone. No family…no friends, just he and his riches and the hired help.

The funeral for this man was sad. I conducted it because he didn't have a minister. It was a graveside service attended by an estranged son and four other guests. I remember waiting at graveside and watching these few guests arrive in their beautiful cars. There was a Jaguar, a Cadillac, and a Rolls Royce Silver Cloud. None seemed to mourn him. They were simply there to pay their respects to a fellow business partner.

Now here I stand in the den of poverty. An oldest daughter conducting a worship service in the front yard, a wife, children, grandchildren, and great grandchildren, filling up the little home. Grandfather's body was in the back bedroom awaiting removal by the local funeral home. The love for him was everywhere. Family members spoke of his great faith and how he had encouraged each of them to become responsible citizens and serve the Lord. One after the other would quote some statement of faith made by the grandfather. His advice to them had seemed to be pure gold. His morning ritual of kneeling at the foot of his bed and praying for his family was known by all of them. It made me want to see this man.

Slowly I walked down the dirty hallway toward the bedroom where the body was. As reverently as I could, I opened the old wooden door to view the remains of an old black gentleman. His hair was white from the years of service. His position caught me by surprise. For there he was, kneeling at the foot of his bed, his knotted hands clasped in prayer, and his head lying on the edge of the bed as if he had not finished his morning conversation with the Almighty.

I told the officer he appeared to die while praying. The officer responded, "He did, Chaplain. He checked out while checking in. Good way to go, huh?"

Good? Good? Good was not a good enough word. Two weeks ago I went to the home where a rich man died. Today, I had come to a home where a truly wealthy man went home to be with the Lord.

I walked outside, took the eldest daughter by the hand and joined her in worship.

~~~

Silver Bullet: It is the heart that makes a man rich. He is rich according to what he is, not according to what he has. -- Henry Ward Beecher

Shield: "Better is a dinner of herbs where love is, Than a fatted calf with hatred. "
Proverbs 15:17

Prayer: Lord, a man's salary was never designed to make a person rich. Nor can riches make a man wealthy. Help me recognize the things I possess that make me a blessed person and to pass them on to those I love.

19

Sometimes It Doesn't Take a Mile to Understand

Friday, June 7, 5:00 p.m.

"Obviously sir, you have mistaken me for someone who gives a s____!"
Joe citizen could not believe what he just heard from a police officer.
The shock was written all over his face! Without muttering another
word, he took his ticket and returned to his vehicle. I had heard officers
threaten to use that remark but had never actually seen the results of
such a statement.

Just a few minutes earlier, J.R. had pulled his patrol car into the
shopping center parking lot. It was July in Oklahoma and hot! VERY
hot! The sun devils seem to dance with glee on the black asphalt
parking lot. We had been discussing the important issues of life. Like
what local greasy spoon served the best hamburgers? Which eating
establishment liked and which ones disliked cops? Important things.
Just as the discussion was about to change to lesser things, J.R. noticed
the sleek, shiny red sports car. What caught his attention was not the
streamlined contours or the fancy pin-striping job. It was something

different. The bright red sports car was parked squarely atop a picture of a wheel chair that had been painted on the asphalt.

Just to be sure, J.R. stopped directly behind the crimson colored vehicle, stepped out of the cruiser into the hot sun, and checked the window for a handicap permit. There was none to be found. Without hesitation, he opened up his citation book and began to write.

A tall young man came running out of the drugstore and up to the officer. "Hey," he said, "what's going on?"

"Did you realize you parked in a handicapped space?" the officer queried.

"What is the fine for that?" asked the young man.

"One hundred and twenty-five dollars, sir."

"One hundred and twenty five dollars!!!" the man shrieked. "That's ridiculous! The reason I am here is because I burned my arm and I needed a burn dressing immediately. That is why I took this spot."

Then came that infamous one liner that took me by surprise. "Obviously sir, you have mistaken me for someone who gives a s____!"

J.R. got back into the car and offered no explanation for his curtness. "I need to run by the house and check on the spouse," he said. "I hope you don't mind."

We rode silently through city streets and finally pulled up to a nice brick home. The yard was manicured, flowers bloomed red, yellow, and white around the sidewalk. He opened the door and the cool air conditioning hit me in the face as I stepped inside. It felt good.

"Pamela?" he yelled. "Brought somebody home to say hi."

Pamela rounded the corner in her wheelchair and said, "Welcome, Chaplain."

Silver Bullet: It is easy to judge people quickly and superficially. It is greater to try to understand.

Shield: For we have not an high priest which cannot be touched with the feeling of our infirmities; but was in all points tempted like we are, yet without sin. Hebrews 4: 15

Prayer: Lord, help me to be able to feel someone else's struggles before I so quickly judge

20

Jesus Wore a Weave

Monday, December 1, 11:00 p.m.

Just a few minutes ago the apartment complex was so different. It was quiet very quiet. The harvest moon set high in the sky and the temperature dropped just to the point of being able to see your breath crystallize in front of you. Night sounds in an apartment complex are different than anywhere in the world. The last stereo has turned down. The last car door has slammed. The neighbor's cat makes its final rounds, and the silver flicker of TV screens shine translucently through the curtains.

Tommy is falling asleep on the couch. He is worn out from being in school all day and his job afterwards. After he got off work at 7:00 p.m., he went by the church to see some of his friends at the youth gathering. Then home and to bed on the couch. The apartment was only one bedroom. His father had been gone for years. His invalid mother lay in bed in the only bedroom they had. Tommy was one of those overweight kids. The kind other kids tease a lot. But he never let

59

that get to him. As he lay on the couch, eyes struggling to stay open, he thought of the upcoming basketball game at the church.

Suddenly, there was a loud crash and a great swooshing sound. A bottle filled with gasoline flew threw the front window and exploded in the living room floor. Local gang members had mistakenly thought Tommy's brother lived there. They couldn't have been more wrong.

Running into the bedroom, he struggled uselessly to get his overweight, invalid mother out of the bed. The tiny apartment began to fill with toxic fumes. His mother shouted, "Go get help! You can't do this by yourself!" Tommy ran to neighbors for help but no one could get back in time. The apartment was engulfed.

When I arrived, the still night was filled with swirling lights, fire engines, police cars, and news reporters. All of them doing their job. Seated on the curb, all alone, in his jockey underwear, feet in the water that leaked from fire hoses, his head in his hands, was Tommy. All he could do was watch helplessly as the remains of his mother were consumed by the flames.

The apartments emptied. People were standing everywhere in the cold night air. I don't remember where the blanket came from that I wrapped around him. I sat down beside him as he told me the story. He was so embarrassed. Fourteen years old with nothing left in the world but his underwear.

I began to ask neighbors for some clothes for him to wear. One man left for his apartment to see what he could find. It was a poor neighborhood. Asking for clothes was asking for a lot. Finally, finding a rather large man, I asked if he had some clothes to put on Tommy.

"Man, I don't own but this set and one more!! What do you want me to do?" The entire time he talked, his breath turned to mist in front of me. For a moment, I lost faith in my fellow man. How could a heart be any colder than the weather.

Easing back toward Tommy, I came upon a young couple. His hair was in cornrows with beads of various colors on the end. He held his girlfriend under his arm as they watched the flames leap into the night. There is no use asking him, I thought. He's probably the very one that threw the bottle through the window anyway. Recognizing my prejudice, I decided to tell him of the young man's plight and ask for his help. I didn't expect him to help. I just didn't want my prejudice to rule me.

In a flash he removed his own shirt and jogging pants and handed them to me. "Here man, I can find some more."

Artists have rendered their pictures of Jesus through the centuries. That night, however, he was a muscular young black man with corn-rowed hair standing in the moonlight wearing only a pair of gym shorts.

$\sim\!\!\smile \smile\!\!\sim$

Silver Bullet: When we listen to our prejudice, we may miss some of the greatest moments God has in store for us.

Shield: "Be not forgetful to entertain strangers: for thereby some have entertained angels unawares." Hebrews 13:2

Prayer: Father, all of us have our prejudices. Help me to overcome them and until I do, help.

21

Life is Seasonal

Saturday, June 2, 5:30 p.m.

The church was decorated beautifully! Each row of seats was marked with a stunningly expensive looking glass globe and candle where they came together to form the center aisle. White satin ribbons hung from each one as if to imitate a breeze flowing through the center of the sanctuary.

The groomsmen, in their black tuxedos, kidded and teased each other as they escorted family and friends to their selected seats. "Bride or Groom?" they would ask as each welcomed guest strolled into the doorway. What a festive day!

The groom was dressed in a white tuxedo. The long tails of his tux gave him an air of aristocracy. Like all grooms, he was nervous. I could see him constantly licking his lips to combat the dryness that accompanied his fluttering stomach. Together with his best man, we sat in a small room awaiting a certain song so that we could make our entrance.

The ushers lit the candles, seated the mothers, and the soloist began her opening number. Then, we entered the auditorium. The air was electric with excitement and enthusiasm. What a wonderful day! I could see the bridesmaids start their walk down the aisle and caught a fleeting glance of the bride as she waited for everyone to get in place and the organist to begin the traditional wedding march.

My mind wandered back several years to the time I first met the bride and her family. They were a wonderful family...very close...very loving. Her brother, Brad, was in his first year of college. He worked for his dad during the summer to pay expenses. Until, one hot summer day, on his way to work, someone failed to stop at a stop sign and crashed into his vehicle. Brad died on the side of the road. One look at the twisted mass of metal told the fatality. But it could not tell the grief it would inflict. Everyone knew his sister, Angie, would take it the worst.

She did.

She loved her brother. They teased each other. They had special nicknames for each other. They watched out for each other. Great sobs welled from inside her as she heard the news. She did not think she could live through this grief.

"Oh God," she said, " I can never be happy again without 'Bucko'." How can I ever have a life after this?"

I remember knowing that things would be alright. That God would have a way of healing and giving life meaning again. I just couldn't find a way to say the words in a believable manner. Her world was crumbling down. She saw no future. She could never picture herself loving again.

Suddenly, I was brought back to reality by the voice of the groom saying, "This would have been Brad's birthday, you know." Angie and her father, Jim, stepped through the door. Both of them beaming with joy. The organ played "Here Comes the Bride!" I smiled knowing that God has a way of bringing life anew.

Silver Bullet: There is no pit so deep that it places us out of the reach of a loving God.

Shield: "For I will set mine eyes upon them for good, and I will bring them again to this land: and I will build them, and not pull them down; and I will plant them, and not pluck them up." Jeremiah 24: 6

Prayer: Lord, let me be comforted in knowing that Your love will sustain me and that You will continually work for good things to come to my life.

22

To Give Reason to Laugh is Love
Giving Reason to Life

Thursday, February 5, 1:00 p.m.

Richard could be loud and obnoxious but he was, most of the time, funny. Upon first meeting him, he seemed a bit ridiculous. Very seldom could you keep him in a serious conversation. He avoided those things. He consistently kept a gag of some kind running at a feverish pace... all the time.

There was the time he stuck his head in the evidence freezer (the one where all the crime samples for homicides, rapes, etc. are kept frozen at 0 degrees). Lowering his head to the bottom of the freezer and placing his tongue on the side, it promptly froze to the top layer of metal and he was stuck, upside down, feet flailing in the air, yelling for help with a hilarious speech impediment due to his latched lingua.

A visiting minister from the community sat in my office and talked of the seriousness of police/community relations, when in walked Richard with a rubber chicken glued to his hard hat! He simply introduced himself in a most serious tone and left.

Richard worked in the lab. The lab was known as the deep dark inner-sanctum of the police department where no normal person would venture. A special group of people work there. Patient, methodical, logistical, temperamental people who spend long hours sorting through mounds of paperwork. Crime scenes to them look like test tubes, fibers, fluids, and microscopic fragments. Yet many crimes are unsolvable without them. Without the badge or the sworn oath of office, they are still policemen, or rather, police people. Good ones!

On one of those rare moments, Richard sat across from my desk and spoke in serious tones. "I just want my life to count for something," he said.

Now, mind you, he was one of the nation's foremost firearm's experts and here he sat wanting his life to "count for something". Admittedly his job did not pay all that well. And, for most of them in the lab, it was a pretty thankless job. He wanted more than just job justification. He wanted to be justified as a person. To be able to say he had worth and acceptance. Like most of us. He had not become the social success he had wanted. He had not become the financial success he had wanted. He was divorced and living in a small condominium.

I explained that value is not determined by what we have acquired but what we have given.

"Do you think I really give anything?" he asked.

"Richard", I said, "you give people cheer in a sad world. You lift burdens, if even for a moment. You make life easier and more fun for people. That makes you count."

Richard died of a massive coronary not long after that. His body was displayed in a local funeral home. What I had tried to say in words was dwarfed by the actions of his friends.

They walked into the funeral home together. It was just prior to closing time. The family had gone home. They were alone. Slowly, they approached the casket and gazed down at a friend. One of them reached into his inside coat pocket, retrieved a special gift, and with tear filled eyes placed a rubber chicken in the foot of the casket.

Silver Bullet: He who spends his life lifting the burdens of others becomes an extension of the Master.

Shield: "Take my yoke upon you, and learn of me; for I am meek and lowly in heart: and ye shall find rest unto your souls. For my yoke is easy, and my burden is light." Matthew 11:29-30

Prayer: Lord, help me remember that when I do something to lift the load others carry, I have touched the heart of God.

23

Helpless People Make Heroes out of Common Ones

Wednesday, July 10, 10:30 a.m.

She lived alone. One of the many elderly people who had long ago outlived their friends and watched as relatives moved away to start new lives in other places. She hadn't owned a car in the last ten years. Age had taken its toll on her vision and decision making ability. She was afraid to drive. A young boy at the local grocery store delivered groceries on Fridays. The local "Meals on Wheels" came by on Tuesdays and Wednesdays, bringing a hot meal and a little company.

The little white clapboard house told of better days. Sitting up on concrete blocks with a crawl space underneath, one could see remnants of grandkid's toys grown dusty from the years of inactivity under the old porch. Placed around the small front porch were old "heating irons", a table knife, obviously used for those times when the keys to the front door were locked in the house, an old teacup that had been sitting on the porch banister for a long time, and assorted flower pots. The rusty screen door was peppered with tiny holes poked in the screen from the scratching of the family pet. An old window unit air conditioner moaned as it struggled to cool the old house.

Life really wasn't that bad. With the help of her walker she could get around the house reasonably well. She often stood behind it at the kitchen sink and washed what few dishes she dirtied... just so things would not stack up. She rose every morning around 6:00 a.m., put on the bargain coffee, fixed a bowl of cold cereal, listened to a local radio station give the traffic and weather report, then slowly got dressed for the day. But the joy of her life was Tony. He was her real friend. Always there, always hanging on every word, always touching, caressing, nuzzling. She literally could not live without Tony. The miniature collie had been with her for years. They had grown old together. She talked with him as if he understood every word and maybe he did. It really didn't matter. He was there. And as long as he was there, she was never alone.

Then one morning, the unthinkable happened. Arising at her normal time, putting fresh coffee in the coffeemaker, with the aide of her walker she shuffled into the living room to find Tony on the couch. He had failed to respond to her call. He simply lay there without moving.

She called again only to learn little Tony had died during the night. He was gone. She cried.

Composing herself, she called the city maintenance and asked for assistance in removing her little friend from the home.

A gruff voice spoke and said, "Ma'am, we don't do that. If you can get someone to put him in a garbage sack and place him on the curb, we can haul him off from there when we make our rounds."

Stunned she simply replied, "Ohhh my, I just don't know what I can do!"

"Sorry ma'am, we just don't do that. That's not our job."

The phone went quiet. She sat on the couch stroking the little dog and wondered if anyone would be able to help her.

The police dispatcher had answered call after call that day. One crisis after another had poured across the phone lines. Big things -- bigger things than the need to move a dog to the curb. But in spite of her already hectic day, something in the voice of the little lady moved her very deeply. There were so many important people in the city. There were so many busy people in the city. People busy with important things. People too busy to haul a dead animal to the curb.

Within an hour of her call, a knock on the door preceded a man with a smile, a small shovel, and a soft blanket. Quietly he entered the small home, placed the tiny animal in the blanket and wrapped him softly. With reverence and respect, the two of them took the little dog to the back yard, silently dug a hole, and buried him there. After placing just a small marker, the man helped the little lady back in the house, said a prayer thanking God for this precious little pal, and bid her "good day."

As he walked out the door, he heard a voice say, "God bless you sir -- and that wonderful dispatcher!"

Silver Bullet: The best days may not consist of accomplishing great tasks but working small tasks for the least of God's people.

Shield: "He that hath pity upon the poor lendeth unto the Lord, and that which he hath given will He pay him again." Proverbs 19:17

Prayer: Father, let me not be so busy that I cannot hear the call of the lowly in their time of need. For in them, I may find You.

24

Faith in Man's Ability is Faulted Faith

Monday, July 1, 11:00 a.m.

The rookies were always ready for Monday morning. It was the time during their training when they left the classroom, strapped on their gun belt, stepped into the sunshine, and began the practice that was the most fun.... firing their weapon. Over and over again they went through the drill. Heat, wind, intermittent rain, the training went on. "Ready on the left! Ready on the right! Ready on the firing line!" Then the familiar hiss of the hydraulic cylinder as the human silhouetted target turned to face each officer. Eyes focused on the back and front sites, grip firm, they squeezed each round hoping on hoping that it would find the target and they would reach their qualifying scores.

This was real cop school. The competition was fierce and friendly. Each one wanted to be "top shot". The adrenaline flowed freely here. The laughing, the kidding, and the feeling of being "real" policemen seemed to be the common thread that tied them all together.

Today was a bit of right of passage day. Each new recruit would be issued his first bulletproof vest. Loosed in this crowd was the sensation of danger and excitement stemming from this initiation into knighthood. The Don Quixote "wanna-be's" stood in line awaiting the acquisition of their body armor. The equipment was state of the art. The best taxpayer money could provide. Lightweight compared to the bulky older ones and less than an inch thick.

One by one the rookies came to the equipment window. Behind the dutch door stood a man in his late fifties taking signatures and issuing the new vests. Tall, sleek, physically fit, white hair and steel blue eyes, Sgt. Kazmerick loved weapons. He knew weapons. A seasoned officer, he listened quietly to the rookies as they talked of how invincible they would be in this new equipment.

"Why, I heard a fifty caliber machine gun couldn't penetrate this new armor.", one was heard to say. On and on they boasted of their indestructibility.

"Hey, Sarge! Give us a demonstration of this new body armor!" one of the more vocal students shouted.

Without saying a word, Sgt. Kazmerick took one of the vests out of the box and walked outside. Cadets swarmed into the sunshine to see the demonstration. The old veteran placed the vest around a large sand bag. The young men and women positioned themselves to be awe-struck by their fancy new equipment. Sgt. Kazmerick reached behind his back, pulled an eight inch butcher knife from his belt, turned and drove it through the vest passing five more inches of the steel blade into the sand bag. Without saying a word, he turned, looked at each officer, and went back inside. The young cadets stood quietly for a while, then walked away.

Silver Bullet: Nothing in life can keep us from needing to depend on the goodness and grace of God.

Shield: "He shall cover thee with his feathers, under his wings shalt thou trust: his truth shall be thy shield and buckler. Thou shalt not be afraid for the terror by night; nor for the arrow that flieth by day". Psalms 91:4-5

Prayer: Father, help me know I must be trained to trust You more than I trust my equipment.

25

Cops are People Too

Tuesday, November 6, 1:00 a.m.

Tamara loved her life as a policeman's wife. Day after day she would listen to Jack's conversation about the exciting life of a police officer. He was her world. She was one of the lucky ones. She had married her best friend. The friendship had simply grown throughout the years. The day began with thoughts of his coming home. They shared so many common loves and even a common faith. God had truly been wonderful to these two.

Tamara sat in the doctor's office and waited for the explanation of her test results. She hadn't been well for some time. Entering the room in his white frock, the balding doctor with friendly eyes tucked behind somewhat thick spectacles, sat down across from her, opened his file folder and said, "Tamara, you have a real challenge. Outside of a real miracle, your disease is terminal."

Tamara rewound the mental tape and played it again. "Terminal! Terminal! That is a scary word, it means DIE!" She sat absolutely quiet and stone faced. With fear in the form of mist that filled her eyes she asked, "Are you sure? How terminal? Uh..Uh... how long?"

"I don't know," came the response. "Weeks, maybe months."

On the way home she debated whether or not to tell Jack. All their married life they had kept nothing from each other, but this was quite different. What was the best thing to do. The front door opened and slammed shut. Jack came in, smiled from ear to ear, and said, "I'm home. What did the doctor say?" She told him. They held each other and cried together.

Tamara looked at Jack and quietly said, "I'm sorry. I wasn't going to tell you. I didn't want to be a burden to you."

Jack listened carefully to her as she explained all her reasons for not wanting to bring such horrible news. When she finished, Jack took her hand, looked her in the eyes and said, "We'll believe for a miracle. Let's just continue to trust the Lord and LIVE!"

Twelve months passed and Tamara grew more frail and weak. Two-day hospital visits turned into two-week visits, with some days filled with the uncertainty of ever returning home. Every day Jack was there tending to her need. For so long she had taken care of him, now it was his turn. He cherished every moment.

Then the day and time came. Tamara was so weak. She motioned Jack close and said almost silently, "Honey, I am so sorry."

Jack paused for a moment then removing the duty belt that held his gun and handcuffs in place, he crawled into the bed with her, boots and all. His strong arms gathered her close and pressed her frail body against his. He whispered, "I love you" and thought, God sent her to walk with me through my life as a cop and He sends me to walk with her now. Tamara died in his arms.

Silver Bullet: Every moment is a time to be cherished for its purpose and promise.

Shield: "Let, I pray thee, thy merciful kindness be for my comfort, according to thy word unto thy servant." Psalms 119:76

Prayer: Thank you for the many ways you send your love to us. May I always recognize how wonderful are Your ways.

26

How Unforgiveness Handcuffs a Heart

Friday, January 5, 9:30 a.m.

"Life just isn't fair, Chaplain." Boy did I know that was right! Any police or fire chaplain would have to whole-heartedly say "Amen" to that statement. Like the wonderful men and women who struggle so hard to protect us, we have seen it all. Life isn't fair. It won't be until Christ is made the supreme judge and ruler of every life.

Bob sat there in my office with both anger and bewilderment etched into his brow. One of his fellow officers had received the promotion he had wanted so badly. But not just any officer. That one. He had gotten the promotion. The one that had indelibly marked Bob's life with hostility and wrathful resentment. For years Bob had felt nothing but indignation for this individual. After all, he had stolen the love of Bob's life. The phone calls, the drop by visits, the awful sense of betrayal to find his wife in another man's arms. No one knew how many nights he lay awake thinking of ways to get even. It ate away at his very insides.

"I know what you are going to say, Chaplain. Forgive. That's what you guys always say. But I just can't let him go that easily. I want him to pay for what he has done. I want him to suffer like I have had to suffer. Besides, I see no benefit in allowing him to get away free."

His huge frame over filled the small chair and he constantly moved to adjust for the uncomfortable feeling both his duty belt and circumstances had placed upon him. His arms were huge and his biceps seemed to stretch the short sleeves of his uniform shirt. His bulletproof vest caused his chest to protrude much like the armor of a Roman soldier.

I rose from my chair quietly and without saying a word, I walked over to him where he sat across from my desk. Looking at his cuff case, I pointed and said, "Take out your handcuffs and cuff me to your wrist."

The huge officer leaned forward, unsnapped the leather case, pulled out the shiny cuffs, and placed one around my wrist and one around his. The familiar clicking sound and the pressure of cold metal against my arm assured me we were securely locked together, "Walk to the door and back." I suggested. As he did I resisted enough to make it more than a little uncomfortable. Several times we repeated the exercise of walking to the door and back with my resistance on the silver shackles.

Finally, I said to him, "Now unlock the cuff from my wrist." Pulling the key from his key ring he placed the cuff key into the little slot and turned the lock. As the silver bracelet fell from my arm, I looked at him and asked, "Now, how many of us are free?"

Silver Bullet: To forgive simply means to "set free from the debt." When you forgive one, two people go free.

Shield: "For if ye forgive men their trespasses, your heavenly Father will also forgive you." Matthew 6:14

Prayer: Lord Jesus, help me to realize that those I choose not to forgive bind to me as I walk through life. And life is often hard enough without encumbrances.

27

Love Lesson From a Child

Sunday, June 2, 7:00 p.m.

Nothing, absolutely nothing, gets to the heart of a peace officer like a child. A child is a living reminder of innocence, truth, justice, and the American way. A child represents all the reasons peace officers put on their uniform and go to work each day. The sight of a little child helps an officer forget about those in the community who dislike cops. It is easy to lose sight of the nobility of the task when you deal with bad people all the time. Who do you trust? Who really is what they appear to be? Every day, one hundred percent of the time, an infant represents those things which are pure and innocent. They are exactly what they appear to be all of the time.

Tony was one of those. Just barely seven years old, he sat in church and watched the visiting minister as he espoused the great truths of the gospel. With a worn, tattered Bible the minister spoke night after night with great enthusiasm. Tony couldn't understand all the words, but he was there. Watching, thinking, planning.

A contest was underway.....a hard one. Any young boy or girl could win a brand new Bible! All they had to do was stand up, in front of the whole church, and say, from memory, the names of every book in the Bible...all sixty-six of them! Quite a task for the older kids. My guess is that the visiting minister could not have done it himself. But Tony was going to try his best.

The meeting was to go for four days. On the third day, Tony told the pastor he would like to give it a try. His insides churning, his blue eyes staring at the sea of people, his spiked blonde hair wet from perspiration, he stood at the front of the church dressed in blue shorts and a striped top.

Obviously nervous and swallowing hard to keep his fear in place, he began... "uhhh Genesis, Exodus, Leviticus, Numbers, Deunaronomy, uhhh, uhhh," On and on he went. Voice shaking, eyes looking at the ceiling, then at the floor. The visiting minister wondered why someone so young would dare go that far out on a limb just to win a new Bible. On and on he went until finally he had named all sixty-six books without an error. He had done it!! In front of everybody. He smiled a huge smile revealing the new teeth that made his baby teeth look too small for his mouth. Tony literally beamed! The crowd erupted in applause. The new Bible was his!

After the service that evening, a small, tow headed, blue-eyed boy came up to the visiting minister and handed him his brand new Bible. "I saw how tattered and torn yours was, I wanted to win this one for you so you could preach from a good Bible. Here, this is for *you*."

~~~~~

Silver Bullet: Sacrifice is never so sweet as when it is made on behalf of someone else.

Shield: "And walk in love, as Christ also hath loved us, and hath given himself for us an offering and a sacrifice to God for a sweets smelling savior." Ephesians 5: 2

Prayer: Father, help me remember the simple joy in giving the simple things in life. For the greater change comes from the giving of a lot of small things over and over.

28

Closing the Gap

Thursday, October 22, 3:00 p.m.

The afternoon shift was just beginning. He walked into the squad meeting, looked on the review board for any new announcements, and said "hello" to his fellow officers. This was his "ticket writing" day. He was anxious to prove that slothfulness was not a part of his character. So he made a mental note to write a certain number of tickets each month. There was only one stipulation. They had to be "good" tickets. Fair, honest, ticket writing. That was the first rule. Even with only a few years on the job, he had already become skeptical of the motoring public. The lies, the innuendo, the outright rudeness had hardened him somewhat to personal feelings. The law was the only safety. Apply the law within the confines of its description and let everything else worry about itself. Never be unfair, but never back down.

He stopped in the men's restroom to look in the mirror and make sure his collar brass was in place and that his cross pen had not been placed through the pocket flap so that it hung outside his shirt pocket. His pants were starched and the stripe down the leg never looked crisper. A quick trip through the car wash and the shiny patrol car was ready for action.

The white police cruiser was filled with sixties music played just below the decibel level of the dispatcher's voice. The officer found his favorite stretch of roadway and pulled his patrol unit to the side of the road just a bit behind a large tree. He took a tuning fork from the glove box, checked the calibration on his radar unit and waited. Within minutes two cars came traveling down the slight incline toward the police car. The radar began to whine and then blink...21 mph over the speed limit!

Locking in the radar display, he stepped out of his cruiser and motioned the first car over to the side of the road. Then began the same conversation that he had heard so many times- "What's the problem officer? You must be mistaken. I wasn't speeding. Are you sure? I really don't think so." The driver continued to insist on his innocence.

The officer kept writing and simply told him, "You'll get your chance to tell it to the judge."

The driver had this happen before. No matter what you say, "the officer is always right." You just couldn't win. After all, he has the badge, the gun, the ticket book, the handcuffs, and the phone number to a dozen other officers should you refuse to play his game.

Don took the ticket book from the officer indignantly, signed the citation, took his copy and handed the book back. As he drove off he thought, "There really is no fairness in this game." Arriving at home he explained to his wife about the ticket and sat down in front of the television to boil in his own anger. "Arrogant policemen!" he thought. "I guess they need the money so bad that they could care less the hardship they cause. I've never known one to admit when he was wrong."

Several hours went by. Don had calmed somewhat as he sat in his recliner watching the evening news. The phone on the end table next to him rang. He picked up the receiver and said, "Hello."

The voice on the other end spoke, "Is this Don?"

"Yes, it is", he said gruffly.

"Sir, this is the officer that stopped you a couple of hours ago. I've been giving that traffic stop a lot of thought. There was a car behind you and I cannot be completely sure that my radar didn't clock him on the incline rather than you. So, I'm calling to let you know that I am marking this ticket void. Please do the same to your copy. Have a good day."

⌒⌒⌒

Silver Bullet: He who offers an apology often gets in the last word.

Shield: "And whatsoever ye do, do it heartily, as to the Lord, and not onto men; Knowing that of the Lord ye shall receive the reward of the inheritance: for ye serve the Lord Christ."
Colossians 3: 23-24

Prayer: Lord, let me remember that it is more important to be gracious than it is to be right.

29

Prejudice Pushed Aside by Producing

Monday, July 19, 09:30 a.m.

Wendy drove down the streets of town and noticed the female police officer directing traffic. She had seen her before and never liked her. What kind of woman would want to be a policeman anyway? Maybe she just wanted to be around men all the time. Whatever the reason, she didn't like her and she let it be known by both her countenance and the way she talked to her friends about her. The officer, Sgt. Susie, knew it too. They just stayed clear of each other.

It was summertime. Wendy was a working mother and her eleven-year-old son, John, filled his days with television and basketball until mom returned home. They laughed together and talked about everything. Wendy's life was filled completely by this young man...her only child...but then...she needed no other. After all, the sun came up and set each day on John. He was a good kid. Never got into trouble. Well, at least not serious trouble.

This particular day, John was shooting hoops in his driveway. The basketball backboard had been mounted to the top of the garage. It banged over and over again as he tossed the ball toward the metal ring and bounced it off the plywood backstop. No one would have guessed in a thousand years what was about to happen. There, in the subdivision, a driver lost control of her vehicle, came up into the driveway, struck John with the front bumper, and carried him through a brick wall as the car passed through the garage.

Miraculously John was alive. His foot was almost severed completely. His body badly crushed and bleeding, John lay just in front of the vehicle with bricks piled around him, someone called Mom.

"Oh my God!" she exclaimed and began driving as fast as she could to be with her boy. Her mind whirred with so many thoughts and so much fear. "Will he die? Who is there with him. He must be so frightened!" Faster and faster she drove. She rounded the corner and nearly fainted as she viewed the damage a speeding vehicle makes as it crashes through your home. She saw the police cars, the ambulance, the people.

"My God, it actually happened!" Wendy, panic stricken and trying to get to her frightened son, jumped from her car, rounded the corner and saw Sgt. Susie. Her uniform bloody, she sat on her knees and held John's head in her lap, stroked his head, and spoke kind, gentle, comforting words into the ears of a frightened little boy as the paramedics performed. That's who God had sent to calm a child's fears in a mother's absence. . . a female police officer. Wendy felt ashamed.

Six weeks later, Sgt. Susie was called into the lobby to meet some "drop in" citizens. The electric lock buzzed as it released the door and it swung open. There in the lobby was Wendy and John. Wendy spoke first.

"We just wanted to say 'thank you' for the wonderful job you do. We really can't thank you enough."

Sgt. Susie looked closely and realized both were on the mend. John from the outside. Wendy from the inside.

Silver Bullet: Sometimes, the best way to answer critics is to produce and keep on producing!

Shield: "And let us not be weary in well doing: for in due season we shall reap, if we faint not." Galatians 6: 9

Prayer: Father people may often misjudge me. Please let it not make me judgmental but let me continue to be Your servant to those that hurt.

30

All Accidents Aren't the Same

Friday, September 11, 7:30 a.m.

McDonald's is a good place for cops. They seem to like it. It may be the festive atmosphere, the bright colors, the bustling of people. But I think it's the free meals some of the McDonalds offer the officers. They seem to appreciate the work the officers do and are always ready to offer a complimentary cup of coffee.

Sgt. Elaine would often stop in there every morning and ponder the activity of the day to come and reflect on yesterday's tasks. Hard work and determination had allowed her to rise to this rank in a short time compared to others. I do not envy women in this field of endeavor. The male ego is very fragile and can often be damaged when a female has proven to be able to do the same job. So even subconsciously, they often don't want a woman to succeed. Things seem to be changing a bit now, but not by leaps and bounds.

The local McDonald's was also the hangout for the elderly men of the community. They gathered together every morning to laugh, talk, and discuss the beauty of days gone by. Often you would see them shake their head in disbelief as one of the orange-haired young people would come into the establishment. You could tell it made them feel left behind in a society where they had no idea how to catch up....nor did they want to.

Bob was the most pleasant and outgoing of the group. He was a genuinely kind, soft hearted, gregarious, and happy sort of fellow. Others surrounded him as he spurred on the conversation rather than take front and center. He would ask questions and call members of the group by name as he called for his opinion. Bob made sure everybody was part of the fun.

When Sgt. Elaine came in, it literally lit up his world. Something about the attractive, outgoing officer made him meet her at the door with a loud "Hello!", a big smile, and a quick hug. He would lead her over to his table, introduce her to the local gentlemen, and insist she sit with them and visit. Sgt. Elaine began to look forward to it every morning. Who wouldn't? It was as if Bob made everybody feel special. His age left him unable to do a lot of physical work, but that wasn't what he did best anyway. He had a gift of giving people acceptance. And in the world of secret resentment and competition, it was most refreshing to Sgt. Elaine.

A few cups of coffee, some good conversation, and a lot of laughs and Sgt. Elaine was on her way. There were school kids to watch, neighborhoods to patrol, and crime and violence to suppress. Driving around that day, she began to reflect on all she had learned as a cop. Some of it really good. In some of the most difficult moments she had remained emotionally detached. She wondered where she got the strength and why it didn't seem to bother her. Was she an emotional cripple or was it because all of these people were just strangers to her? What kind of person had she become?

The radio cracked and the dispatcher sent her to a traffic accident at 151st and Peoria. It was a common place for a traffic accident. People just couldn't seem to get it together at that intersection. Just a few months before, she had found a young man lying dead in his pickup after running it down a ravine at that same place. She wondered what it would be this time. Would she need to give CPR? Would the ambulance already be there? Would she need to summon the fire department? Her mind whirred as fast as the siren as she drove upon the scene.

The large Ford pickup had failed to yield the right of way. As a result the truck was struck in the side and rolled. The driver was lying face down next to the vehicle. Elaine was the first to arrive. Seeing that driver number one was in fair condition, she called for an ambulance and rushed to driver number two, who was still lying face down and not moving. Her heart pounding in her ears, she carefully rolled him over to bring his face out of the grass and into the air. Her heart literally stopped as she recognized the driver. It was Bob. The same Bob she saw every morning at McDonald's. The same friendly, smiling, cheerful Bob that greeted her with such warmth. He didn't look right here. He was not supposed to be on the side of the road with his insides a crushed mass.

She got down on her knees and formed a lap in which to lay Bob's head. He opened his eyes and his steel gray eyes met hers. A slight smile formed on one corner of his mouth as he recognized her. Then, in a moment, while being held in her arms, he died. He was there and then. . . he wasn't there. So quick. So fleeting a moment that one had no time to capture the moment anywhere but in the recesses of a caring heart. That is where that moment will stay.

Elaine called the coroner. Inside she hurt incredibly. So many accidents, yet this one was so different. She really hadn't changed that much. It was just that, today, the victims became real people. People that will always be loved, always be missed, and always kept alive in the quiet corners of the caring heart.

The task now is to care while continuing to work. . . to help when your heart cries in sorrow. That too is a cop's job. You have feelings. You have cares. You also are called to do a wonderful noble task. To put aside your grief until the job is done...then know you too are human.

Silver Bullet: The most important thing in life is not the triumph but the struggle. The essential thing is not to have conquered, but to have fought well.

Shield: "We know that we have passed from death to life, because we love the brethren. He who does not love his brother abides in death." I John 3:13 (NKJV)

Prayer: Lord, You know more than I how much I love this job. In my effort to do my best, allow me to love… for in that is life. Let me not become so attuned to the task that I miss your treasure in people. Let me live and not just be alive.

31

Creativity Among Concrete Guidelines

Friday, July 15, 1:00 p.m.

"Creative law enforcement" -- now there's a term every police officer has heard before. Every decade is credited with something new to add to the law enforcement know-how. Ron Taylor was no different. A cop of the 60's and 70's, he had his own way of dealing with things. But only since his retirement would he admit to some of them. And I want to emphasize some of them.

For instance, there was a creative way in dealing with the sea of indigent personnel staffing the bridges, libraries, and rail yards of the city of Tulsa. Most police officers spell the word indigent. . . WINO. Believe it or not there are a lot cops who would love to help these individuals. However, the needs of the indigent seem to far surpass the officers' ability to help. Up until Ron, their only resource was to chase them to another block of the city or arrest them and take them to jail. And believe me, that can get very old.

At the time, not many agencies wanted to help the indigent of the city. At the same time, they didn't want them hanging around the rail yards, the libraries, and under the bridges. One night, in the wee hours of the morning, Officer Trenton walked through the rail yard again. He stumbled upon an unconscious individual he had arrested time and time again. The Night Train Express bottles beside him told the story. Looking at the open and empty boxcar and without waking the individual, Ron loaded the middle-aged man into the car, closed the door, and walked away. When asked how he handled drunks from then on, Ron simply said, "I give them an all expense paid trip to Detroit or wherever the train happens to be going that night."

There were other ways of creative law enforcement. For instance, in years past, when the jail needed a cook for the inmates, the dispatchers would let the police officers know. Many of the officers were well acquainted with the town drunks. They knew which one could cook and which one couldn't. They simply went to the areas that were familiar flops, found a cook, arrested him for public intoxication, and the city had a free cook for 30 days.

Sergeant Neil Chesney was creative in his method of law enforcement also. His meticulous method of report writing earned him the nickname, "Neat Neil." Even more unusual, Neil often held prayer meetings before the normal squad meeting, where it earned them the name "God Squad."

On one particularly hot July day one of the members of the God Squad was called to a local furniture store. It seemed that a mentally disturbed individual had entered the establishment, informing everyone that the devil was leading him, and started throwing furniture through the plate glass windows. This type of call immediately brought the supervisor, Sergeant Neil Chesney.

Some of the strongest people you will ever arrest are those that are mentally disturbed. It seems their strength is endless. This individual was shouting obscenities, threatening lives, and throwing furniture. The proper procedure was to go in with guns drawn, demand the individual to drop the furniture and go to the ground. A brass ashtray on a brass stand can be a deadly weapon in the hands of a mental patient. Sergeant Chesney ordered his men to stay outside the building. He removed his duty belt and all his weapons, entered the building, came from behind, and grabbed the raving individual.

Locking his arms around him, Neil began to whisper in his ear, "God loves you. He's here with you. He is stronger than the devil. You can trust Him. He has defeated the devil that is trying to ruin your life. God loves you." Then Neal began to pray, "Father, I ask you to bring peace to this man. Help him grow calm so we can help him."

As strange as it sounds, the man began to grow peaceful. The expression on his face changed, his voice became softer, and he surrendered himself to Sergeant Chesney. He was then transported without incident to the local mental hospital. Maybe you've never thought of getting God involved in your job. Perhaps you're working harder than you need to.

<hr />

Silver Bullet: Life is not an easy matter.... You cannot live through it without falling into frustration and cynicism unless you have before you a great idea which raises you above personal misery, above weakness, above all kinds of perfidy and baseness. - Leon Trotsky, Diary In Exile, Entry for April 3, 1935

Shield: "I will bring the blind by a way they did not know; I will lead them in paths they have not known. I will make darkness light before them, And crooked places straight. These things I will do for them, And not forsake them." Isaiah 42:16 (NKJV)

Prayer: Lord, give me new, creative, and safe ways to do this job. I invite You into this task with me. You place in my hands the power to deal with people, the good, the bad, and the troubled. May your wisdom teach me how to deal with each one.

32

Cops With Feet of Clay and Hearts of Gold

Thursday, February 15, 4:30 p.m.

I've known a lot of Christian police officers throughout the years. Many of them made loud verbal professions of faith, while many others made loud living professions of faith. I have to admit, when I started this job I thought the best Christians were the ones that were the most vocal. After twenty six years of this, I have decided that probably the best Christian police officers are not the ones with loud voices proclaiming their faith for television, radio, and the local church establishment. But rather, they are the ones that live day in and day out following the principles of Christian character and life without making a lot of noise.

It almost seems that it is the young Christian who makes the loudest noise, and the older, more seasoned ones, that live quietly day after day doing their best. And believe it or not, I think I know the reason why. You would have to be a part of law enforcement family to understand what the pressures are really like. The personality type that is attracted to this job is usually one looking for a new adventure, excitement, and the thrill of the moment. It is also a very noble mentality that seeks to help people. When you place yourself on the cutting edge of life, the affirmation of doing a good job is imperative.

The male police officer is often subjected to women who admire his job, maybe looking for some sort of protector, or just simply attracted to a uniform. When a heart searching to be a savior finds one filled with admiration, both seem destined to fall for each other. I'm sure that is an over simplification. However statistics prove the divorce rate among law enforcement personnel are some of the highest in the nation.

Neither is the female officer immune. It is incredibly difficult to enter an occupation that doesn't think you belong. It takes a strong woman not to seek the acceptance and approval of her peers. And it's not the loud boisterous police officer that gets approval. It is usually the kind, quite, strong one that causes them to stumble. One officer stated, "All men are wolves. Gentlemen are just wolves with patience."

The Christian officer with the loud testimony and the pushy attitude has yet to discover the weakness in the human flesh. But rest assured he or she will. I cannot and will not give correct names here. I remember one officer who used his uniform to obtain speaking engagements in the local churches. His Christian testimony was very loud and flamboyant. After finding his wife was unfaithful, he was charged with battery of his spouse. "Tom" was very active in his local church, openly encouraged all the officers to call on the chaplain for help, and was incredibly ashamed when caught in an affair. There was "James" who lost his job due to alcoholism, "John" caught stealing from the property room, and "Peter" who denied three times that he knew the Lord.

Each of them made radical statements about their faith, yet were unable to live the radical lifestyle that it called for. None of which is surprising! I have been a Christian for almost forty years and can still preach more Gospel in ten minutes than I can live in ten years. The point being, that we should live a quiet and simple life and trust much in the grace of God.

Lewis sat in my office with his eyes cast down as if he were watching ants crawl across the floor. Up until now, he had been very vocal regarding his faith. Now he was hurting, ashamed, and feeling completely alone. He had committed the big sin. The grandmother of all sin. The most embarrassing of them all. The big "A"!

He said, "Chaplain, I don't know if I can get through this one. It wouldn't be so bad if everybody didn't know. Even my church people know. Even the officers I have witnessed to know. I screwed up really bad. I have really let God down. He must really hate me. I have completely stopped going to church. What can I do?"

"Lewis", I said, "you have already done the most important part. You have recognized you were wrong and have agreed with God. I'm sure you have asked his forgiveness over and over again. Now, instead of acting caught, act forgiven."

"How do I do that? I can't go back like I was! No one would take me seriously! I am too embarrassed to go back to church. I'm just stuck!", he said.

"Not unless you want to be. Don't isolate yourself from God or from the people He wants to use to help you get through this. Would it not be strange if, when we were sick, we refused to go to the doctor until we were well? If you crashed your patrol car, would you refuse a paramedic until you are no longer injured? Of course not! You would know that these people were there to help put you back together again. The true Christian officers that are here will work with you and support you. The others never did anyway. If the church you attended cannot extend to you the grace and mercy necessary for healing, then find another one, but don't stop going. And lastly, allow God to use this to teach some of the deeper more healing truths. Lewis, we all know how to act like a sinner. Stick around and show us how to act forgiven."

∿ ⌣ ∿

Silver bullet: What makes humility so desirable is the marvelous thing it does to us; it creates in us a capacity for the closest possible intimacy with God.   -- Monica Baldwin

Shield: "Dear brothers, if a Christian is overcome by some sin, you who are godly should gently and humbly help him back onto the right path, remembering that next time it might be one of you who is in the wrong." Galatians 6:1 (NKJV)

Prayer: Father, until I have fallen so far as to break my pride, I have yet to fall far enough. Teach me to be gentle and forgiving to both others and myself, for we all both belong to You. Help me to act forgiven until I feel forgiven. May humility keep me at the feet of Jesus.

33

Take Yourself Too Seriously and Nobody Else Will

Wednesday, December 19, 8:00 a.m.

His laugh was one heard around every squad room. A thundering guffaw punctuated at the end with a loud "Woooooooooo!" He's been around a long time. "Mossbacks" they are called. In fact, he was often kidded about being the one who took the original report involving the Cain and Abel homicide. He wasn't always that way, though. Many remember him when he took both his job and himself too seriously. As a young officer, he seemed to believe God had commissioned more than one Savior. He viewed every assignment as one with dire consequences and the world teetered dangerously on his shoulders. But through the years, the job had a way of enlightening his consciousness into a "not so serious" attitude.

In earlier years, he was a motorcycle cop. You know, the one with the knee-high leather boots, the tight riding trousers with the stripe down the side, black leather jacket, and that polished gold helmet? Sitting behind a bush at the end of the street, engine off, radar on, he tracked the oncoming, ever elusive, vehicular prey.

Out of the corner of his eye, three houses down, he noticed one of the elderly citizens exiting her front door and, with the help of her aluminum walker, step down onto the sidewalk. Their eyes met and she turned to walk slowly toward him. Preparing for his upcoming "Atta boy" speech, he straightened his leathers and sat a little taller in the saddle. After all, he was a police officer. One of the finest the city had to offer. Of course little old ladies would want to visit with him. He removed his mirrored sunglasses so that he would not look so intimidating.

"Sonny," she said as she got closer, "I sure appreciate what you wonderful boys do, but could you at least TRY to hit the front porch with the newspaper from now on? It's hard for me to walk all the way across the front yard."

Realizing what had happened, he simply smiled and said, "Yes Ma'am, from now on I will do my best." Pressing the starter button, he roared to the next location.

Silver Bullet: Learn to take your job, but not yourself seriously. Laughter at oneself plants the seeds that produce a long life and a fulfilling career.

Shield: "Laughter doeth good, like a medicine." Proverbs 17:22 (NKJV)

Prayer: Lord, help me learn that You have everything in control. Help me to, in my job, do my best; and laugh at the rest.

34

God Can Wear Green

Friday, September 23, 12:30 p.m.

Suicides are rarely reported in the news media. Unless it is particularly tragic, it never makes the evening, or even the morning, broadcasts. This one made it. Partly because a two-year-old child was involved. But mostly because it happened across the street from the local NBC affiliate.

Lorraine's life had been marked with one failure after the other. Alcohol had carved its woeful initials all across her existence. Failed marriage, failed occupations, failed motherhood were all part of her recent history. She was preparing for another court appearance for DUI, Driving Under the Influence. This would be her fifth one. It could even carry jail time in the state penitentiary.

The sun beamed through the windshield of her car while the cool breeze of her air-conditioner whisked across her face. Her son sat quietly seat belted in the front seat. Between them was a small purse that contained the answer to her guilt and shame. Her car rounded the corner into the subdivision and her small brick home surrounded by large trees appeared in view. The car bounced up the driveway and snapped forward and backward as she placed the car in "park" a little too quickly. Stroking the hair of her little boy, she unfastened his seat belt, took her purse, and led him up the sidewalk and to the front porch of their home.

Reaching inside her purse, she moved aside a large steel object and located the keys to the front door. Unlocking the door, she placed the young lad inside, kissed him on the cheek and said, "Mommy is going bye-bye. Be a good little boy."

With that, she quickly closed the door, removed the large steel object from her purse, placed the barrel in her mouth, and pulled the trigger. As the hammer struck the firing pin, the gun performed flawlessly. Her life hurled into eternity in less than a second.

The scene was soon inundated with news media, neighbors, firefighters, police officers, and sightseers. All were focused on the limp body lying on the front steps. If ever there was a place where God needed to be seen at work, it was here.

Few ever noticed the female police officer just out of view of the rest of the crowd. She had been one of the first to arrive. In her arms she held a very confused and frightened two-year old boy. Approaching the scene moments before, she had simply stepped over the lifeless body, scooped up the terrified little guy, and dedicated herself to taking care of just him. Eyes glassed over from the pain, she talked softly and encouragingly to the fellow.

It was the worst day of his life. In that day, God sent an angel. Dressed in a uniform and a badge, arriving in a swirl of red and blue lights, God's angel took him into her arms and said, "The hurt stops here. Enough hurt for one day. Now you are under my care."

Silver Bullet: The caring hands of God may often be at the end of a uniformed sleeve. Through you, he can bring the hands of the greatest Healer to the greatest hurting.

Shield: "Then shall he answer them, saying, Verily I say unto you, Inasmuch as ye did it not to one of the least of these, ye did it not to me." Matthew 25:45

Prayer: Lord, I will see some of the most hurting in the world. Let my hands become an extension of Your own as I reach out help in some small way.

35

Pauper with a Purpose

Friday, November 29, 9:00 a.m.

The fire seemed to explode in sections across the open field as the wind blew it faster and faster toward the waiting homes. One by one residents watched helplessly as their trailer houses, workshops, and frame homes were transformed into black smoke, then transported into the heavens. Each a sacrificial offering to the fire demon that cared little for the children and parents left with no place to go.

As I stood in the middle of the meadow that birthed the destruction, my eyes were so caught up in the devastation that I failed to notice one small, two-room home left unscathed in the middle of it all, and one lone individual, stumbling and walking toward me. He had seen my Chaplain's jacket and seemed extremely excited. He flailed his arms in an uncoordinated fashion as he motioned for me to stay where I was. When he finally got to me, he began to speak in words that were slurred and hard to understand. Cerebral Palsy had taken its toll on both his coordination and speech. Seeing that I could not comprehend, he began to pull on my coat sleeve, leading me toward the tiny dwelling.

It was green and the asbestos shingles said that it had been green a very long time. The porch consisted of two steps that lead you inside a wood frame shanty. A swinging light bulb suspended from a cord, ignited by a pull chain, gave all the light that 75 watts could muster. His kitchen, bedroom, living room, den, and study were all the same room. Though clean, it was old...very old. The old man had built shelves on every wall of the one room and had filled them with some of the finest theological works I had ever seen. I had to struggle hard to understand him.

I pointed to the books and asked, "Why?"

His eyes, though gray, were alive with excitement. I had obviously asked the right question. He pointed to a bulletin board above the desk. Pictures and letters filled the board. A black phone and an answering machine that looked completely out of place sat atop the tiny desk.

Slowly and with great difficulty, I began to make out the words.

"I don't have much." He said. "and people can't understand me when I talk because I have Cerebral Palsy. But I do have faith that God can understand every word I say. So…I pray for people every day. They call me with their prayer requests and I put their letter or picture on my prayer board. I study these books so I will know how to pray for them … and did you see? Did you see where the fire went? It burned up to my house. It burned my yard. It even burned under my house. But IT DID NOT BURN MY HOUSE! This is GOD'S HOUSE. It is my prayer closet and I MUST COUNT WITH GOD, 'cause He would not let my prayer closet be burned!" His eyes danced, his contorted smile spoke volumes.

How lucky he is, I thought.

Silver Bullet: The poorest of all men is not the man without a cent, but the man without a dream.

Shield: "Where there is no vision, the people perish." Proverbs 29:18

Prayer: Lord, help me not to live for the praise that flows from human lips but for the voice of Jesus that simply says, "Well done, thy good and faithful servant."

36

When a Cop Becomes a Convict

Tuesday, February 5, 10:45 a.m.

Driving toward home, my mind was a thousand miles away from the world of law enforcement. Merging into the freeway traffic, I turned the radio up a little louder. I sang along with Sam and Dave as they did a rendition of "Midnight Hour." "Man, where did this music go?" I thought. Sensing a familiar vibration along my belt line, I reached down, unclipped my pager, and gazed at the display. Hmmmm, I had just left the office.

What could they want? Grabbing my radio, I pressed the phone line button and placed the call back to my office. "Chaplain, can you come back? We are about to arrest one of our officers. Will you meet us in booking?" My heart sank!

Gaining clearance through the booking area, I viewed the pale green walls with the same discomfort experienced so many times before. Yet this was strangely different. A long wooden bench sat on one end of the room. It looked peculiarly like a pew removed from one of the local churches. The only real difference was the steel eyehooks imbedded in various locations. Placed there to secure prisoners in hand cuffs during the booking process.

Having viewed prisoners seated here many times had not prepared my mind for such a dejected sight. Walking into the room under the scrutiny of security cameras, my eyes looked into the fear struck, shocked, and shameful gaze of a police officer cuffed to the wooden pew. A bright cheerful countenance had been replaced with a paled expression where the talons of trauma had etched deep lines. He spoke to me as if his head had been dizzied by a blow. His words were slow and lethargic.

Blank eyes filled with tears gazed at nothing when he said, "I can't believe this. I just can't believe this."

With no words of comfort coming to my mind, I sat down beside him, placed my hand on his shoulders and said, "Here is where we have to trust the Lord. God doesn't give up on us."

He had no idea he was even being investigated for a crime. He was summoned to the internal affairs office and asked for his service revolver before any explanation was given. The arresting officers were not untouched. Their pain was easily apparent. They were embarrassed, sorrowful, and stunned at the turn of events. To arrest and book their own was as traumatic an event as they would ever experience. They needed God's comfort as well!

Months passed. Sitting in my office one day, I received an usual letter. It went something like this:

Dear Chaplain,

I can't thank you enough for being with me that awful day. It seemed life simply got out of hand. I didn't wake up one morning and decide to commit a crime. A man's actions do not go out of control. They GROW out of control!! I now realize it is the correct handling of our small failures in life that secure us from the big ones. Discipline in small areas keeps us from paying this price for failing in big areas.

Silver Bullet: Things are either right or wrong, not right or alright.

Shield: "Let my soul live, and it shall praise thee; and let thy judgments help me." Psalms 119:175

Prayer: Lord, you know my failures better than I. I ask and receive Your forgiveness for where I have wronged You, others, or myself. Give me Your strength to overcome them one day at a time.

37

This One Thing

Monday, July 8, 10:00 a.m.

It was late afternoon at the firing range. Jeff knew he had to make a certain score or his career as a cop would be over before it even started. He wanted it more than anything. He would pay any price to get to wear that uniform. He had studied his written material and had done well, so far. Now it was down to qualifying here.

Round after round had been discharged at the human shaped silhouettes. The July sun bore down hard and sweat poured like buckets from the brows of the recruits. Each one struggled to improve their skills to meet the strict qualifications placed before them. They would begin at the seven-yard marker, then progressively retreat until they sighted at the target fifty yards away.

Jeff was having a particularly hard time. Due to previous surgery on his hand, the weakened ligaments made it nearly impossible to squeeze the trigger with the proper finger. In an effort to compensate, the rookie was sneakily using the middle finger to apply the pressure needed to discharge the semi-automatic weapon.

While they struggled in the summer sun, I sat in the air-conditioned tower with one of the instructors. Inside the almost soundproof glass room, we could visit as he watched each recruit on the firing line. Pop, pop, pop, the guns fired over and over again. As we talked, he took a pair of binoculars and closely observed the rookie's form.

"How are they doing?" I asked.

"Fair for the most part," he stated. "I'm about to wash one out though! That one right there." He pointed at Jeff.

Realizing that such a short statement in an air-conditioned tower could have such long- reaching results I asked, "Why?"

"Well, just watch what finger he is using to fire that gun," he said. "He's trying to circumvent the training. When I asked him if he was doing that he told me, 'No, sir'."

Clamping down on his chew of tobacco, he stated his case. "You know, all we ask them to bring to this academy is a willing heart and honesty. We can teach them everything they need to know to be a policeman. We can give them the tools they need and the education necessary, but we cannot give them a willing heart and honesty. That one will wash out, not because we can't teach him to be a cop, but because he is short on honesty."

Jeff never got to wear that uniform.

∿‿ ◡‿ʌ

Silver Bullet: A person becomes honest when he strives to fool no one, even himself.

Shield: "He that hath clean hands, and a pure heart; who hath not lifted up his soul unto vanity, nor sworn deceitfully. He shall receive the blessing from the Lord, and righteousness from the God of his salvation." Psalms 24:4-5

Prayer: Lord, I have made so many mistakes. I need Your forgiveness and Your strength. All I can offer You is a willing heart and an honest admission of my weaknesses. Thank You, that it is enough.

38

Salvation from a Shot

Tuesday, March 9, 5:00 p.m.

"Well, boys, I think I'll try to serve this felony warrant on ole Larry. Anybody want to go with me?" It was a pretty common warrant. He had served a lot of them. The procedure was simple. Go to the door, knock, when the door opens, ask for Larry and tell him he will have to go with you. That's the way most of them worked. This one didn't.

Alan would never impress you as a poster boy for the "I wanna be a cop" campaign. He laughed easily and loud. His uniform was not the tailored cut shirt. His hair never had the "military" look or the "styled" appearance. His trousers were not pressed as sharp as those who spent hours preparing to meet the public. In fact, he carried his gun belt lower than the rest, as if it just couldn't' quite find where the waistline was supposed to be. You could not help but like him.

Joking with his partner, he knocked on the door of the small home. The suspect opened the door and, viewing the two officers, slammed the door and headed toward the back room. Impulsively, Alan swung the door open and ran inside. Standing in the front room of the residence, gun drawn, he yelled for Larry to come out into the hallway. The officer began to move cautiously into the hallway, looking in every direction, heart pounding in his ears. The room was virtually alive with sounds. The tiny squeak of his hand tightening around the grip of his service revolver, the heat and air unit running, and his own breathing combined to make deafening noises pulsating in his inner ear.

Like a flash, it happened. The figure stepping out of the bedroom, lowering a shotgun at the officer in the hallway. No time to think. No time to yell. No time to pray. Just before the shotgun fired, Alan discharged his weapon -- a burst of fire from a stainless steel barrel.

A bluish gray smoke filling the hallway, leaving a smell as if a roman candle had just been ignited. A roar that drowned every other noise in the room sent a projectile tearing into the flesh of the upper thigh of a man now dropping his weapon. The lead missile severed the femoral artery, a lifeline. Bright red blood literally spewed onto the floor. Doctors would later state he had only a few minutes before he bled out and died.

Then something happened that forever changed my view of law enforcement. As his partner summoned the emergency medical service, Alan holstered his weapon, walked over to the dying man, placed his hand over the wound and asked God to stop the bleeding and spare his life until he had a chance to receive Christ as his personal Savior. I don't know if you believe in miracles or not. All I can tell you is that the bleeding from the femoral artery began to subside. The medical team arrived long after he should have bled out. Surgeons stated the only way to slow the bleeding would be to stick your thumb into the artery and clamp it off. There, kneeling beside him in a pool of blood, Alan led the man in a prayer inviting Christ into his life.

Later, Alan, and other officers would go to the hospital room and conduct private Bible studies for him. National Geographic magazine featured the story.

Silver Bullet: He who thinks traditionally can only rise to levels already reached.

Danny Lynchard

Shield: "For he is the minister of God to thee for good. But if thou do that which is evil, be afraid; for he beareth not the sword in vain: for he is the minister of God, a revenger to execute wrath upon him that doeth evil." Romans 13:4

Prayer: Lord, there are many ways I can be your servant and do this job. Lift my thinking until I think the thoughts of God. Until I see with Your eyes and serve as Your hands.

39

Faith Works by Love

Tuesday, November 21, 8:30 a.m.

Things were quiet in the office. The phone rang and the voice on the other end of the line was unrecognizable. "Chaplain, this is Alma. I live in California and I am looking for my son. I haven't seen him in years but I need to find him desperately." Her voice quivered and cracked as she tried to solicit help from a stranger. She went through agonizing detail describing how her son had always worked for little or nothing trying to help people less fortunate than himself. She had records that could place him in every state between California and Arkanss. "His brother has died. He hasn't seen him in ten years. He needs to come home and I have no way of finding him. Can you please help?"

She described her son, Roland, age forty-three, married, but never owning a telephone. He often lived in housing provided by non-profit organizations so as to be close to people he could help. He had even considered the ministry at one time.

The tedious search began. With only his name and date of birth, the long task of making phone calls and entering computer databases began. As far as I could tell, he never had a driver's license, owned a car, listed a telephone, or had utilities placed in his name. State after state was contacted for any record. No arrest record, no felony record, not even a speeding ticket! It was beginning to look hopeless. Alma never gave up. When I would grow tired of searching, the phone would ring and it would be Alma on the other end asking about results.

Three days passed. The funeral for Roland's brother was conducted without Roland. Alma grieved not only for a lost son, but for two lost sons. One to the grave, the other to the countryside. "He MUST know!", she said. "He must."

On the day after the funeral, Alma located his social security number and called with the new information. She hoped this would be the bit of data that would help locate her son. At 8:00 a.m. she called to give me the number and encourage me to keep trying. Hearing the pain in her voice, I hung up with a new resolve to try again. I literally prayed, "Oh God, help this woman find her son. She needs him so and he needs to know his brother has passed away."

That afternoon, Alma answered a knock on her door. It was Roland! She couldn't believe it! All these years!!!! With no knowledge that any life-changing event had taken place, he had begun a cross-country hitchhiking trip from Tulsa, Oklahoma to his home in California the day after his brother passed away! "Momma, I just had a desire to come home."

Silver Bullet: Hopelessness belongs only to those who believe everything depends on their own efforts.

Shield: "Are not two sparrows sold for a farthing? And one of them shall not fall on the ground without your Father. But the very hairs of your head are all numbered. Fear ye not therefore, ye are of more value than many sparrows." Matthew 10:29-31

Prayer: Lord, help me remember there is nothing out of your sight or your control.

40

Quittin' Time Will Come

Thursday, December 7, 11:00 a.m.

Standing six feet tall and two inches, full faced and barrel chested, he had a smile that would draw you to him but eyes that made you believe he was setting you up for embarrassment. His mannerism always kept people off balance in his presence. Maybe he planned it that way. I'm still not sure. He was confident. Never ran with the pack, yet managed to be admired by most of his coworkers. He was probably the most intelligent traffic cop I have ever known, though some of the brass would call that a contradiction in terms.

And....he lived and breathed police work. It was his life and light. It gave him a reason for his existence. He could find a "probable cause" for a traffic stop in less than a half a block. He was current on all law changes, D.U.I. testing techniques, and traffic accident analysis. He used it to brag about his ability to determine fault. When asked how he would fill out a certain accident report, he replied jokingly, "First, I decide whose fault I want it to be." When a small department could not budget a radar unit, he bought his own. On his fortieth birthday he wrote one citation for each year of his existence. Not one was contested in court.

I saw him recently. Still six foot-two but no longer his full faced, barrel-chested self. Physical illness was responsible for a loss of body weight. His hair was thinner, the lines that marked his winning smile were trenched a little deeper, and his eyes seemed to try to hide how he really felt. No longer able to "do the job" he seemed to be searching for his position in life. Somehow, he had lost his way. He was .. no .. he **is** a cop. He just can't play the game anymore.

"What are you doing now?" I asked "Oh, working on my next position as a CEO!" he chirped. His smile invited laughter but his eyes simply said, "God, what I would give to get in that uniform and chase the bad guys one more time!"

It is great to find joy in your job. It is another to find your reason for existence.

Silver Bullet: Who you are as a person and what you do as an occupation can never be combined as one in a healthy manner. Integrity, honesty, sincerity, and caring are things that define a person and can be carried with you wherever you go.

Shield: And now abideth faith, hope, charity, these three; but the greatest of these is charity.
I Corinthians 13:13

Prayer: Lord, help me realize my job today is to be a Christian. Allow me to find great satisfaction in simply letting You live through me.

41

Reaching In to Reach Out

Monday, May 15, 7:00 a.m.

Confused and burdened, Jim drove his car uphill on a two-lane road. At the top, he turned his vehicle around, pulled to the side of the road and looked back down the hill toward the innocent looking intersection. Through a corridor of telephone poles he tried to visualize a small blue pickup driving downhill toward the intersection -- the young driver, late for work, never noticing the stop sign or the vehicle approaching.

Two weeks earlier Jim had sat at the breakfast table with his son, Brad. It was threatening to rain. A light mist had already begun to settle on Brad's gold Trans Am. Hurriedly he placed the T-tops on the beautiful gold car, slid into the driver's seat, fired up the throaty engine and left for work. He worked for his dad's office supply store and attended college. He was bright, witty, and full of fun. Like kids should be. When he approached that intersection, he never saw the small pickup rapidly approaching on his left. With a thunderous crash of metal and glass, the small pickup slammed into the driver's door of the Trans Am, diverting it off the road and into the embankment.

The pickup flipped end over end, dumping its eighteen-year-old driver head first into the concrete abutment. Both kids died instantly.

Just after the Medical Examiner left with the lifeless bodies, a van pulled up to the crash scene. Recognizing the gold Trans Am, the van driver stated to the nearest officer, "That's my son's car. Where is he? Where is Brad?" hearing the truth, he searched each face as if trying to find someone to tell him it wasn't true. There was none. Leaning back into the doorway of his van, sliding down to the running board, he looked up and asked a power packed question, 'What do I do now?"

Though appearing to be a very practical question, it had futuristic overtones. As if to say, "What do I do with the rest of my life, now that Brad is gone?"

Now, two weeks later, he sat viewing the intersection. He struggled to understand why this terrible thing had happened. He resolved that he would write his feelings down in an effort to help others facing similar tragedies. Page after page flowed from his hand as he spoke of his anger, his confusion, his hurt, and horror. But during the process something happened to Jim.

As he prayed for answers to give people during their grief, a real healing started taking place in his own heart. Slowly, taking three steps forward and two steps back, he became more at peace with what had happened. He began to be able to put the blame aside and actually came to a day where he could be happy again. As he searched for answers to share, God gave him courage to bear the burden that had robbed him of his own son. He became a walking expression of dignity and determination ... of caring and courage.

⌁～ ⌣⌒⌁

Silver Bullet: Sometimes, when personal problems seem to overwhelm us, we may find the solution by becoming involved with the hurts of others.

Shield: "Look not every man on his own things, but every man also on the things of others. Let this mind be in you, which was also in Christ Jesus." Philippians 2:4-5

Prayer: Lord, I do have my own struggles and I thank You that Your concern for my good is greater than my own. Help me empty my hands by placing my problems in Your hands. For only then can mine be free to help others.

42

A Christmas Like No Other

Monday, December 25, 5:30 a.m.

Green Country Oklahoma can be quite beautiful in the wintertime. Cover the leafless trees in a thin sheet of ice and throw six inches of snow on everything and it truly is a picturesque place. The buzz of a powerful saw pierced the silence of Christmas morning. Hundreds of feet of plastic pipe running underneath the river bridge had been charred by a 2 a.m. fire. Probably set by a transient trying to stay warm on this freezing winter day. A large portion of the city had lost its phone service as a result.

Huge bundles of plastic pipe carrying phone lines and other public service from one side of the city to the other were attached to the underside of the bridge. The crawl space between pipe and concrete made a perfect home of hibernation for transients finding themselves alone and cold on Christmas day. Thousands of motorists would cross that bridge during the week. Few knew what was underneath the bridge or why the loud drone of a chainsaw could be heard coming from underneath it on this most holy Christian holiday.

Utility workers fated the task of removing the damaged pipe and cable and replacing it with new. The workman's saw, cutting through the plastic tubes and exposing the layers of pipe, gave them the appearance of looking down the multiple barrels of an old Gatlin' gun. The old saw groaned loudly as it cut through the last of the pipe. Debris flew through the air and something large, something human, cascaded down onto the chest of the phone repairman.

Glancing at the steam coming from around the object, the worker stared in disbelief. No arms, no legs, and only four inches of vertebrae sticking out of the torso where a cranium should rest . . .all that was left of some homeless individual trying to find a way to stay warm.

Wearing protective gloves, the detectives sifted through all the debris, one small piece at a time, looking for the rest of the remains of Mr. John Doe Homeless. A uniformed officer stood close by. It was Christmas morning. Both had families. They could have been angry. With scowled faces, irate words, and bad attitudes, they could have fulfilled the obligation that brought them a paycheck.

But, instead, with warm smiles and a hearty, "Well! Merry Christmas!" they greeted me. They both laughed easily and joked about being under this bridge on Christmas morning. So much so, that to the untrained eye, each would have seemed untouched by the gruesome task facing them. Their laughter belied their sorrow for one lonely, unidentifiable, misfit, sleeping under a bridge. But I knew them. I knew how lucky we were to have them. I knew that John Doe Homeless could not have had two more sensitive, concerned, professionals at the site of his demise. Their appreciation for life, all life, and the recognition of the worth of a human soul were unsurpassed.

As I left there, I quietly prayed, "Lord, bless these wonderful people." Somewhere, deep inside my spiritual person, a voice seemed to assure me that He would.

Silver Bullet: Sometimes the audience that views what we do consists not in the greatness of numbers but the greatness of ONE. Hallowed by the name of the Lord!

Danny Lynchard

Shield: "And whatsoever ye do, do it heartily, as to the Lord, and not unto men; knowing that the Lord ye shall receive the reward of the inheritance; for ye serve the Lord Christ. " Colossians 3:23, 24

Prayer: Lord, help me to do my job today as if I am doing it just for you.

43

If You Lie to Anyone, Let It Not be You

Tuesday, September 17, 2:15 p.m.

He had been hard on life. Looking at his dark hair, youthful face and winsome smile, one would never guess burglary, armed robbery, and drug trafficking were a part of his history. Young, good looking, bright eyes, and quick to smile, Bobby seemed to have it all together again. Life had not been hard on Bobby. Just the opposite. His parents were not wealthy but had provided for him well. Only his private rebellion could explain the path he had taken.

With eyes that danced as he spoke, he told me all three of the biggest lies told in prison. "You will never see me in here again. I have found the Lord, and I am going to stay away from my old friends." How many chaplains, parole board members, and police officers have heard those same lies? Like so many others before him, Bobby lasted about six months before he was back in the same prison.

I had believed him too! Some of my acquaintances had gotten him a job and secured him a place to stay. Now, I looked into those eyes again. No longer dancing. No longer full of excitement. His open shirt revealed a scar on his stomach where he had tried to stab himself with one of the prison spoons.

Everything seemed to turn bad so quickly. A night out with friends where Bobby refused drugs but did take a drink for "old time's sake?' After all, he was a Christian and he had changed his life. He was strong now. One month later, he was standing at the back door of a local pharmacy with a screwdriver prying open the door lock. Inside was his precious treasure...and the local police.

Now, peering from behind bars again, Bobby was truly disillusioned in himself. Like a bolt from the blue the truth struck. Bobby had lied to himself. He didn't know he was lying. He thought he had it all together. He really believed all those lies. Just like the rest of us! Bobby was simply caught up in the pride of life. He had judged himself by his "intentions" not his actions. He fooled himself by himself. What a shame.

Silver Bullet: It is not how we act when people notice but what we do when no one is looking that accurately registers our character. Pride will deceive, but the truth will set us free

Shield: "Pride goeth before destruction, and an haughty spirit before a fall." Proverbs 16:18

Prayer: Lord, teach me consistency. Help me be the same person whether alone or in a crowd. Forgive me when I have trusted in my own strength and, with Your words of grace, show me the new person You have created in me.

44

Helping from the Heart

Thursday, June 13, 2:40 p.m.

Psychologists have studied the making and profiles of serial killers. Those committing the most heinous crimes have earlier accounts of cruelty which predict even more serious things to come. Typical of this is cruelty to animals. At age seven, Jeffrey Dahmer gave his teacher a bowl of tadpoles. Infuriated that she gave them to a friend of his, he sneaked into the garage and killed them by submerging them in motor oil. His fascination with savagery to animals is well documented.

As a child, serial killer Ed Kemper buried his family cat alive, exhumed, beheaded it, and reburied the animal. If those type of detestable acts point to the darkness looming in the heart of an individual, then surely the love, respect, and kind treatment of the least in God's kingdom must point to the light that shines in an individual reflecting the goodness of God.

Dancer had just about lived his life out. Thirteen years is a long time for a miniature pinscher. But a good dog can put a lot of love, loyalty, and levity in his remaining years. His steps were not as quick as the young pups around him, but his loyalty and love had a depth that pups would know only after years of living. His miniature pinscher features gave him the look of a yuppie dressed in motorcycle leathers. The small black figure appeared to be outlined in a medium brown. His eyes, pointed ears, mouth, tummy, toes, and tail were highlighted in what appeared to be caramel. At the sight of its owner, it seemed that all the little dog's joy would build up in his stump of a tail and could only be dispersed by vigorous wagging.

The fire caught suddenly that day. The home was filled with smoke and flame in no time at all. The owner was able to get out with only herself intact. All her worldly possessions, including Dancer and two other younger dogs were left inside. The bright red fire truck rounded the corner. You could hear the diesel engine rev as it sped toward the residence. Fire fighters jumped from the truck like babies leaving a mother spider going in every direction. Some pulled a fire hose toward the home. Others pulled toward the hydrant. The owner cried for her animals trapped in the inferno.

Firefighters began to soak the burning home. A dragon was now captured in a single-family dwelling and was shooting huge flames through the windows. Black and brown smoke billowed into the air while tongues of fire taunted fire fighters daring them to come inside. One of them did and re-appeared with two of the scared creatures . . . but no Dancer. To go inside a burning structure that could collapse at anytime and bring two of three out is a wonderful gesture of good will and bravery. It should be enough. Dancer was an old dog. He didn't have many years left anyway. Two out of three should be good enough. From the fringes of fire the owner pleaded with them. The little dog had been her constant companion.

Inside, Dancer had succumbed to the smoke and heat. His lungs filled with hot fumes, his little body dehydrated from the heat, his eyes unable to see, his little legs no longer able to carry him, he dropped to the floor and prepared to die. Quick shallow breaths and half-opened eyes were all that was left.

The light coming through the front door pierced the smoke and outlined a looming figure approaching the tiny canine. Seeming to float through the haze of smoke with an oxygen tank and clear full facial mask, the silhouette looked more like a diver approaching than a firefighter. Strong gloved hands reached underneath Dancer and picked up the little limp body.

As the two broke into the sunlight only a single paramedic noticed the small form drooping over the hands of its rescuer. Having endured all this, Dancer appeared to be gone. Grasping the tiny tyke in her arms and hurrying him away from the now engulfed home, the paramedic did what she had been taught to do to save a tiny life. She placed the oxygen-pulse monitor on his thimble-sized foot and adapted the oxygen mask to fit Dancer's miniature muzzle. His face had the pall of death. She was an animal lover, but this time it seemed too much. Then she felt a slight squirm of life. Two shiny bewildered eyes opened. The petite little pooch began to recover. Everyone cheered as Dancer was placed into the arms of his tearful owner.

The beloved dog that her son gave her one Valentine's Day many years ago is alive and well. Dancer's a little slower, but she's certain he'll be able to enjoy the twilight of his life dancing along to country and westerns songs – the same as he has since he was a pup. It was a great moment.

Somewhere in America, someone is being cruel to the smallest and most vulnerable of God's little creatures. Today, two 'someones' saved the life of one of them. Each act a reflection of the kind of people they truly are. Not surprising the latter wore uniforms of public service.

Silver Bullet: The calling of God is deeper than a call to specific tasks. It is a call to specific meaning and purpose. It is revealed in the way we interpret our duty.

Shield: "Keep your heart with all diligence, For out of it spring the issues of life."
Proverbs 4:23 (NKJV)

Prayer: Lord, I want to be Your instrument of help to the hurting I see today. I ask You to help me serve from my heart for it is there Your greatest wisdom is revealed. It is there Your greatest love can be understood and it is there You live and visit me.

45

Officer Osmosis

Tuesday, June 17, 3:00 p.m.

My first time with an officer! What an education! As a rookie police Chaplain, I guess the thing that surprised me most was the officer's nonchalant ability to ask the people with whom he dealt some of the most personal questions "What's your name? What's your social security number? Where were you born? Why is your husband upset? Have you been drinking? Have you ever been arrested?" I always felt as though I was invading their privacy with those questions, but to a police officer its just part of the job.

When we walked into the booking area, there they sat. Three young tan-skinned disheveled males waiting their turn on the breathalyzer. Eyes red and glassy, speech slurred, and "a strong odor associated with intoxicants on or about their person." They stared angrily at us as we walked in. Looking at me, one yelled, "What kind of cop are you dressed in a suit?"

"I'm not," I said, "I'm the chaplain." I fully expected the same reverence I was accustomed to in other circles.

"Chaplain! A preacher! I don't want no damn preacher in here staring at me."

Trying to calm him, I said, "Sir, I'm not here to stare at you."

"Then get your ass outta here, damnit!"

Shocked and embarrassed, I was speechless. I felt so belittled. I dropped my head and sulked out of the room. That incident weighed heavily on me. Walking into the booking area two weeks later, the memory was still very vivid. A tall, slender male, dressed in a suit, with his tie loosened, sat where the others had sat before. The same red eyes, the same slurred speech, and the same question came back to me, "Who are you with that three piece suit?"

As calmly as I could, I walked over to him, checked his handcuffs, took his tie in my hand, pulled him up close and said, "I'm the new district attorney and if you don't want to LIVE here, you better button it up!"

Life and the people you meet can change you. Sometimes for the better. Most people won't believe that, but it does. It can build strength of character and a faith that is increasingly stronger by facing the challenges placed before you. Or, like me in the aforementioned, it can make you intolerant and uncaring.

It depends upon whose strength you are leaning – yours or a higher one.

~⁓ ⌣ ⌣⌒⌃

Silver Bullet: Good fruit is grown by what it draws from the roots, not the atmosphere

Shield: "I am the vine, you are the branches. He who abides in Me, and I in him, bears much fruit; for without Me you can do nothing." John 15:3

Prayer: Lord, help me not to judge people I meet on the merits of people I have met. Let me allow each to stand on his or her own merits. Help me to allow tolerance and forbearance to be part of my everyday life.

46

God's Gavel

Sunday, May 25, 7:00 p.m.

Don't beat your prisoners. Don't falsely accuse. Don't complain about your pay. Three edicts for law enforcement officers straight from John the Baptist. Sounds pretty easy, initially, doesn't it? Except for the pay part, it really isn't hard to comply with such expectations. Beat a prisoner? No way! After all, you are an understanding person. Wit and reason are your friends. Simple commitments to logic will keep you from crossing that barrier. But believe it or not, in police work the most even-tempered may, at times, find it a difficult mandate to keep.

Jake was a simple bad guy. He didn't have a high IQ. He was not a master thief. He wasn't even a good one. He had been arrested so many times that most of the local officers recognized him on sight. Often, before the ink was dry on the paperwork, Jake was back out. At age 35 he had already served time for burglary, armed robbery, assault and battery on a police officer, and forcible sodomy. Yet he walked the streets every day basically a free man. The mention of his name made the temperature of injustice escalate immediately to the boiling point.

Now he had done it again. Driving along a city street in the hours just around daylight, he noticed an eleven-year old girl seated at a bus stop. Quickly he pulled to the curb and forced the startled little girl into his vehicle. Driving her to his garage, he repeatedly did what he was famous for, then drove her back to the bus stop and pushed her from his car. Shattered and ashamed, she told her story to the officer.

Driving the city streets, the officer played the crime scenario over and over again. Finding it hard to remove the voice and face of a frightened little girl from his mind, he turned his radio to an oldies station and tried to sing along. In his peripheral vision he noticed a man walking quickly down the sidewalk. Turing the corner to get a better look, he locked eyes with Jake. The pursuit was on. He pulled the police cruiser to a sudden stop and lurched from the driver's seat. Chasing him on foot down an alley, he drew close enough to throw his weight into the center of Jake's back. The two went crashing to the ground. As Jake resisted, the officer placed his knee on the nape of Jake's neck, wrenched the assailant's arm as high up behind him as he could, and cuffed him. Now it was just he and Jake alone in the alley. Just he and Jake…no judge, no jury, no parole board, no lawyers, just the memory of a frightened little girl and Jake.

He tried desperately to control his anger. At times like this, righteous indignation, that primal cry for justice, rises uncontrollably in all of us. His better judgment struggled to remind him that his job was to take people to justice, not justice to people. Yet his emotions were confirming the opposite.

Still sitting astride his prisoner, the glint of the badge on his uniform caught his eye. A sharp reminder that it was not in his job description to seek the destiny of either the innocent or the guilty. A different justice would prevail.

Jake would live to meet his.

〰〰

Silver Bullet: Try to remember, the final sentence doesn't come after a man has lowered the gavel, but after God has lowered His.

Shield: "Vengeance is mine, I will repay saith the Lord." Romans 12:19

Prayer: Lord, help me not to look to man and his system for justice. Keep me ever mindful that true justice, as true grace, lies only in Your grasp. I trust You.

47

The Biggest Battle

Wednesday, September 24, 11:00 p.m.

Not many people in our department do not remember Bob Fagan. Controversial? Yes. Unorthodox? Definitely! Caring? Without question. A little crazy? Probably so. But he was also a lot of what good officer are made of. A Vietnam veteran standing well over six feel tall, this guy looked like the poster boy for "I wanna be a cop." More than once he had placed himself in excessive danger to apprehend the bad guy. He had spent hours upon hours and dollars upon dollars trying to help those forced to live in the alleyways and side streets of his city. A House of Prayer for local winos was repaired and affectionately nicknames "Fagan House." But none of us talk about Bob much. I'm reminded of Dan Akroyd's statement on *Saturday Night Live Re-Union*. When speaking of the late John Belushi, he said, "Those that knew him know the real truth; those that didn't will never know."

Suffice it to day that Bob Fagan fought a lot of battles from inside a uniform. His biggest ones were inside himself. One night, in the basement of the police garage, Bob ended the conflict. A two-page note was all he left behind. His years of feeling like he could never do enough came to a cataclysmic end. One of my greatest honors was the day his parents presented me with his casket flag, badge, and medals. I still display them in my office.

Why? Because Bob represents a lot of officers. Officers that go out to give it all they've got, yet find the job is never done nor is as fulfilling as they had hoped. Like Bob, all of us want what we do to make a difference. We seem to find acceptance and approval based on the success of a job well done. But police work is often performed by faith. Successes are usually intangible. Remember, when you're a police officer, you always get there after the fact. You can't determine how many accidents, rapes, murders, or robberies you prevented. You spend most of your time reporting failures.

And at the end of the day, the biggest battlefield of life is usually within yourself.

~~~

Silver Bullet: Many talk of God saving us from sin. Not enough talk of how He can save us from ourselves.

Shield: "So you see how it is: my new life tells me to do right, but the old nature that is still inside me loves to sin. Oh, what a terrible predicament I'm in! Who will free me from my slavery to this deadly lower nature? Thank God! It has been done by Jesus Christ our Lord. He has set me free." Romans 7:24,25 (Living Bible)

Prayer: Lord walk into my battlefield with me, whether it be filled with enemies that know me not, or with personal struggles that know me all too well.

48

Dealing with the "L" Word

Friday, December 5, 9:30 a.m.

Love. What a mushy word! It's not a cop's word. Or at least not one that is used too seriously among the rank and file on a day-to-day basis. Often it is connected with romance or some other "feminine" thing. When you look people in the eye, that word can be the hardest one to say. Yet the Scripture commands that we do it. Love, that is.

But I have seen love in the field. Many times the word was never used but it was quite visible. Like the time one of the sergeants bought a new bicycle for a kid on his beat. Or the special donation taken to buy an electric wheelchair for the spouse of a fellow officer. You see, love is a verb…an action word. It is something you do and it counts the most when it is done for those who cannot repay.

Bob had pulled his cruiser into the driveway of one of the more humble neighborhoods of the city. "Check on the well being of the children," was all that had been dispatched. The cold December wind bit into his collar a he walked up the broken concrete sidewalk and knocked on the door. Inside he found a mother and four children with no heat, no running water, and no winter clothing. The children, enamored by his presence, looked in awe at the man in uniform. One ran and clasped his arms around the calf of his leg and said, "Hi, Mr. Policeman!"

The radios in all the cruisers were quiet when Bob's voice broke the squelch. "Does anybody have any winter coats?" That was all he said. The conviction in his voice was enough to motivate many of the offices to find winter clothing and bring it to those children. That, you see, is love. In a non-sterile environment, filled with want and need, pure love can came in the same hands that cuff a criminal and fire at a felon.

It's reflected in the actions of the officer who spends a little more time on the report in order to get all the information; in asking the victim not only "How did it happen?" but "How are you doing?" or writing a traffic citation while treating the violator with dignity and respect.

In short, love is a verb. It is what we do IN SPITE of how we feel sometimes. Even then it is not doing what the object wants, but what will make them a better person as a result of having met you.

Silver Bullet: Love is work. It is not "working on your feelings," it is doing the right thing for the right reason.

Shield: "Love worketh no ill to his neighbour: therefore love is the fulfilling of the law." Romans 13:10

Prayer: Lord, make me an instrument of your love today. Give me the insight to see that I can make a difference. And in my giving, help me accept Your love for me.

49

When Humanity Becomes Holy

Friday, November 15, 10:00 a.m.

The damp, dark, musty crawl space underneath an old house was the perfect place for spiders, scorpions, snakes, termites, and other creepy crawlers, but it was not the place for little boys. Yet there he was, just over a year old, severely beaten, tiny head swollen from being thrown against a wall, wind pipe all but sealed shut from the screwdriver that had been jammed down his throat….handle first. Placed there by an enraged adult. An old carpet was tossed over the small quivering body in an effort to conceal what was thought to be a lifeless little boy. He was left to die.

Oz had been missing since before dawn. The chill of early spring made everyone wear jackets in the morning and long-sleeve shirts in the afternoon. Now, a small group of police officers stood around the abandoned house trying to decide who would craw through the small opening of the enclosed crawl space to find the remains of the little boy. The lot fell to the smallest officer, a female. Her mission, check every inch of the crawl space in search of the body of Oz Dacatur.

Stepping into her white overalls and putting on her gloves, she pointed her flashlight under the house and squeezed through the small opening. Sometimes crawling, sometimes pulling her body along the ground, she moved toward a pile of mildewed, smelling carpet. Removing the carpet, Officer Cindy Luke was stunned to find the child's body. The shock increased even more when she heard a faint whimper escape across his tiny lips.

At that moment a transformation took place. A transformation that lifts people from job descriptions, responsibilities, obligations, and duty fulfillment into the ranks of real loving human beings. For at that moment, Oz was not just a victim and Cindy was not just a police officer. Each became something more…something higher.

The officer radioed to the waiting partners that she had found the infant but he was barely alive. Paramedics were summoned. As she waited for their arrival, the officer placed her cheek against the child's cheek, molded her boy to his to keep him warm, and there, under an old abandoned house, asked God to save the life of little Oz Decatur. Now there were three under that house. An officer, a child, and a loving God, summoned by the prayer of an individual who sought to do more than just follow policies and procedures.

Oz came out from under an abandoned house and survived against all odds. Newspapers and television followed his progress. Citizens pitched in and brought toys, food, clothing and gifts of money to help with expenses. Large churches with beautiful auditoriums and magnificent altars continued to pray for the child's recovery.

Yet none were as powerful as the one whispered in a little boy's ear underneath an empty house.

~⌣ ⌣ ⌒

Silver Bullet: There is nothing glorious about dying on a cross. Nothing noble about crucifixion. Yet when it became an act of love for mankind, it elevated a terrible tragedy into the greatest triumph the world will ever know. Nothing counts more than those sacrificial acts of love, but in order to do them, we must allow ourselves and those around us to become real human beings.

Shield: "And they went to him, and bound up his wounds, pouring in oil and wine, and set him on his own beast, and brought him to an inn, and took care of him." Luke 10: 34

Prayer: Lord, help me make the big difference by caring a little more. Protect my heart as I offer it in prayer to those in need.

50

A Little Child Shall Lead Them

Friday, August 22, 1:30 p.m.

Ten-year-old Nesha started in the shallow end of the swimming pool and began "swimming" to the other end. The only uncertainty... Nesha couldn't swim. Half way into the deep end she began to struggle, kicking her little legs and flailing wildly as her ten-year old cousin, Tanya, began to encourage her to "Hurry, Nesha, hurry! Keep trying! You can make it!" Nesha went under and sank to the bottom. Tanya jumped in but couldn't reach her. She ran to the apartment complex looking for help but couldn't find anyone. Breathless she returned to the pool and couldn't see Nesha at all. The newly refurbished pool was too murky from the chemicals to see clearly. Tanya thought she had gotten out. Slowly she walked back to the apartments. This time she located some adults and told them what had happened. Jumping into the pool, one of them found little Nesha's body on the bottom, still in the deep end.

CPR efforts ailed. Emergency crews raced Nesha to the local hospital. She was pronounced dead, and one by one the family began to arrive, including Tanya and her eleven-year-old sister. The hospital room seemed so cold as Tanya and her sister marched down the hallway and asked to say goodbye to their dear friend and cousin. Tanya silently sobbed as she and her little sister viewed the tiny lifeless body. Nesha's feet were crossed, her hands folded on her tummy, and her eyelids were almost half open.

Tanya's little sister was incredibly cute. Her pigtails dangled around large eyes, surrounded by beautiful ebony skin. She seemed far too young to be in this room looking at her departed cousin. The little girl looked at me and said, "Her eyes are open. Is she really dead?"

"Yes, dear, she is," I responded.

"What happened to her? Did she swallow too much water?"

Taken a little aback by such innocence, I said, "Yes, yes, you could say that's what happened."

"Is she ever coming back?" she queried.

I thought for just a moment and said, "Not for a long, long time, because she is in heaven with Jesus and He loves her very, very much."

Her eyes widened as she asked one more question. "She is in heaven? Right now?"

I smiled and said, "Yes, she is in heaven right now."

The little girl grabbed her sister's arm and said, "C'mon, Tanya, Nesha will be jes fine!" And with a wave of her hand, she said, "Bye Nesha," took her sister's hand, and the two of them left the room.

Silver Bullet: Oh that we may have the faith of a little child.

Shield: "And he said, Verily I say unto you, Except ye be converted, and become as little children, ye shall not enter into the kingdom of heaven." Matthew 18: 3

Prayer: Father, help me learn the difference between being naïve and having simple child-like faith.

51

A Touching Transformation

Thursday, October 3, 11:00 a.m.

The phone rang. "We have some abused children coming in for
a statement. There will need to be pictures. Would mind being a
witness?" Gathering my coat, heading out the door and into the night,
I wondered what would transpire over the next hour.

The officer in charge was, Susan, a female. Trapped in a world
of male-dominated tasks, she often reflected a very tough exterior. It
must be hard to find acceptance where smaller men would never wish
to succeed. Men who belittled your accomplishments and highlighted
your weaknesses in an effort to prove this job should be "For Men
Only." But she had done it. Achieving the rank of Sergeant, she was
in charge of child abuse cases. Noting her tough exterior personae, I
hoped she could really work with children.

It was my first time to witness such statements. Sitting in a little
isolated office two rooms down from the entrance, gazing at light
yellow walls and nervously waiting for the alleged victims to arrive,
I found my eyes focused on the carpet while my mind sought to find

a way just to get comfortable. Why are police walls always yellow or green or light blue or mixture of the two? Couldn't they make it a little less cold and indifferent?

Then, through the doorway, escorted by a uniformed officer over six feet two inches tall and weighing close to three hundred pounds, came two little wide-eyed boys. Except for their scared faces, they actually appeared as little leprechauns alongside the giant of a man. They looked like little stair steps. Their hair was cut into a flat top, so short you couldn't tell whether it was blonde or light brown. Little skinny legs stuck out of baggy shorts that extended way past their knees. They reminded me of pictures I had seen of my own youth. They were brothers. About ten years old – they had shared a lot of things that brothers should share – the capture of strange bugs that invaded the neighborhood, exploring open park areas in the summertime, bouncing their first basketball. They also shared the beatings – beatings that left them cut, bleeding, bruised, and worse, terrified. Many a night they cried each other to sleep, dreading the moment they crossed the line for another one. Now they clung to each other as they were forced to expose their family secret and share the degrading experience of taking their clothes off in front of strangers and allowing them to photograph the most private parts of their anatomy.

The officer left them with me. I tried to make them feel easier, but to no avail. Their eyes look at me like trapped little animals forced into submission. Without choice, without dignity, insecure, afraid and alone, they stood in that cold office with only each other.

Then Susan walked into the room. A bright smile, eyes dancing at the sight of the young boys and with a cheery voice called them by name and, although she had never met them, talked as if they were old friends. The room actually grew warm as she made even me believe she was more interested in them as human beings than she was in the crime that had been committed against them. She asked them about school, their favorite sports, and what they enjoyed most. She made them feel they had value, real worth! It was almost magic as two young victims were transformed from statistics to status. What a difference! They talked. They smiled. They laughed. With a God-given gift, she was able to transform children who, more than once, had been beaten into frightened submission as evidenced by the deep bruises on their backs

145

and buttocks, into radiant, talkative, outgoing, intelligent young men. It was a miracle! Somehow she made the whole thing "all right."

A police officers greatest work may not be to bring in the bad guy, but that moment when he or she stopped all the law enforcement and made a victim feel like a human being again.

$\sim\ \smile\ \wedge$

Silver Bullet: As an authority figure, your words have great power. Use them to build something good in those that choose to hear.

Shield: "Take my yoke upon you and learn of me, for my yoke is easy and my burden is light." Matthew 11:29

Prayer: Lord, help me to be more like Jesus. Help me to find ways to be a burden lifter so that I may bring Your touch to the hurting I see each day.

52

Let Laughter Lighten the Load

Monday, May 11, 8:00 a.m.

Simply sitting in his office was an experience. On his desk was a computer filled with information about numerous makes and models of handguns, shotguns, and rifles. Placed on his wall was a display of every cartridge every produced by Winchester Corporation. Under the microscope were the spent rounds taken out of the body of a mother recently killed by two juveniles. As she walked out of a clinic with her two children, she was accosted and shot for the contents of her purse... less than $10.

Searching the rifling, firing pin indentions, and pressure points could tie the weapon in question to the victim. More evidence to assure these two would never do such a thing again.

Day after day, hour after hour, case after case, he would fire weapons into a vat of water, analyze the projectile, and find similar markings to match weapon to crime to person. He was one of two firearms experts in that state. You can imagine how many sad stories he had heard. But people seemed to like Richard.

On the edge of his desk was a reproduction of the human skull. He had spring-loaded the jaws so that they could hold his outgoing mail. He had devised a hinge so that the top would flip up and the cranial cavity was filled with hard candy. Everyone was encouraged to help themselves. As strange as it sounds, this seemingly warped sense of humor was what endeared people to him. His simple ability to smile was contagious. It made people want to be around him.

Coming into the Emergency Operations Center lobby, there is a security camera attached to the ceiling and focused on the elevator. One day, walking around the corner, I caught him standing behind the camera making clucking noises as he held a rubber chicken in front of the lens and walked him back and forth. With blushed cheeks and a mischievous smile on his face he simply placed his index finger to his lips and said, "Shhhhhhhhhh".

Richard got into a bike riding club. He thought he would improve the looks of those spandex shorts he wore, so he put a potato in his pants . . . . in the back! When Richard died, all of us mourned the loss. Friends lined up to view him for the last time. Some of his family placed special objects in the casket to be buried with Richard. . . things than meant something to them. I watched "Tom" slip something in the casket and slide it toward the bottom. Very few people ever knew what "Tom" placed there. I did. . . . . a rubber chicken.

Cops see enough bad in the world that is it easy to become negative. This one knew the antidote.

Silver Bullet: People prefer shouters to pouters. Smiles will bring things your way that will eventually make you feel better. Frowns turn people around; smiles draw them to you.

Shield: "Laughter doeth good, like a medicine." Proverbs 17:22

Prayer: Lord, help me to remember to bring positive things into peoples lives today. Knowing that we shall reap later what we sow today. Let me sow a merry countenance.

53

Forgiveness in the Face of Death

Sunday, November 22, 9:30 p.m.

John was only thirty-seven. He spent the last two years of his life in one of those sleazy motels where police officers often find working drug labs. You know, the type of motel that desperately needs a paint job and the management will rent a room by the week or hour. For more than six months John had lived on what the community could provide him through its charitable organizations. He knew how to work the system. He often sat in the dimly lit room watching a television screen that was no longer in color or black and white. The characters on the screen now looked almost alien, with their skin and world tinted green.

It wasn't really what the room contained that made it such a sad place. It was what it did not contain. It didn't contain proper lighting, family pictures, or his wife of eleven years. It had never seen his daughter or his mother and father. John didn't even know where they were . . . at least not for the last ten years. And now the tiny room contained even less and less of his life. He was dying. Every day a little more of his life seemed to drain away. Blood slowly oozed from his most private places as the executioner called "cancer" ravaged his body. The Gideon bible he found in the nightstand made him want to talk to someone about God, his past, and his parents. He reached for the once beige colored telephone, now darkened by the oil of so many palms, and dialed 911. He was transferred to me. He was crying when I answered the phone.

In a broken and tearful voice he threw away the veils of false pride and deceit in an effort to expose the desperateness of his situation. The end of his life so close in front of him made the past appear all too clearly. It nearly crushed his soul. If something didn't change, and soon, he would die all alone in a cheap motel in Tulsa, Oklahoma. His last wish was to locate his father and mother and somehow obtain their forgiveness for the life he had led.

We talked for about a half an hour. I took the sketchy information about his family and could offer little assurance of finding them. People's lives change a lot in ten years. They relocate, divorce, secure unlisted phone numbers, or even die. I really had little hope of locating them. I spoke sincerely and asked, "John, if I do reach them, what will I tell them to assure them I am truly representing you?" His answer was both astonishing and sad. "Tell my mom the biggest a--hole in the world wants to talk with her before he dies." He assured me there would be no question in her mind I was legitimately calling on his behalf. How sad! John's biggest concern would be her unwillingness to talk with him.

We prayed together over the phone and asked God to help me locate his mother and father. I hung up the phone and went to work. After several hours of records locating, internet searches and chasing down blocked alleys, I dialed one last phone number. A very kind voice answered on the other end. I went through my now normal presentation. "I am sorry to bother you, maam. My name is Danny Lynchard and, to be honest, I don't even know if I have the right phone number. I have been asked by John Stevens to assist him in locating his mother and father. Do you have a son by that name?"

There was no noise on the other end of the phone. "Maam?" I said. Her voice was so soft I could barely make out the words.

"Oh my God! We have been looking all over for him! I've prayed and prayed that we would find him. Where is he?"

"He is here in Tulsa, Oklahoma. He lives in a motel. I have a phone number."

She was crying now as I related the whole story. The gift of forgiveness had long been extended. She only awaited the opportunity to let him know. I hung up the phone feeling I had been a part of some great miracle God had been designing for a long time. I hurriedly dialed John's number. In a run down motel, an old beige telephone rang and John answered.

"John, I have found them. I talked with them."

John began to cry aloud. Cavernous cries . . .the ones that come from deep inside the chest of a man. Finally gaining his composure he asked apprehensively, "May I call them?"

"Better than that, John. They want to come and take you home with them."

Silver Bullet: God loves you much more than even your earthly parents. His forgiveness has already been extended. You only need to contact Him to receive it.

Shield: "If you then, being evil, know how to give good gifts to your children, how much more will your Father who is in heaven give good things to those who ask Him!"
Matthew 7:11

Prayer: Lord, help me to understand just how much you are willing to forgive and accept me. May I lose sight of my past by bringing You into my future.

54

Who is my Neighbor?

Tuesday, October 26, 1:45 p.m.

His name was James Krispus. When he came into the Day Center for the Homeless, no one wanted to be around him. He stood only five feet and eight inches tall. His skin was darkened more by dirt and filth than by the sun. He made his home underneath the railroad trestle where Main Street and Archer meet. As homeless people wandered around the large open room, James sat alone at a table scratching his arms, his back, his legs, and other places too private to mention. His incessant scratching finally caught the eye of Lori, one of the social workers at the Center.

The slightly overweight angel of aid approached his table slowly and sat down across from him. "Hi, I'm Lori. I know that you are new here and the director has asked me to see if there is anything you need."

"No! I just need to be left alone!" His eyes widened and looked more of fear than anger. James suffered from severe paranoid schizophrenia and had not been on medication for a long time. His paranoia and mood swings made him a dangerous man and often quite unpleasant. He had no friends. His family had long given up on trying to help him.

Lori was able to give him a change of clothes. She took his old ones to the medical department to determine what may have caused the continuous itch that led to continuous scratching. The result was the finding of a type of parasite larger than a head louse yet smaller than a mosquito. The report read, "an extreme infestation of a sucking type of louse found mainly on pigs and horses."

There are those people who will die and no one will care enough to realize they are gone. Officers have found bodies that have laid dead for days, weeks, or even longer. Not because of foul play, but merely because the deceased was endeared to no one. The scent of a strong pungent odor or someone accidentally stumbling onto the corpse would be the only catalyst for contacting the next of kin. James was sure to be one of those.

Bob Tubal was the conductor of a Burlington Northern Railroad train. Twice a day he passed over a particular trestle. Each time he would blow his whistle and the man living underneath it would come out and wave at the conductor of the huge engine pulling the long line of cars. Though they never officially spoke, a real fellowship seemed to develop between the two. In the morning the train would pass over, sound his loud horn, the old man would come out and wave, and Bob would wave back. The procedure was repeated a few hours later on the return trip.

On the morning of October 26, Bob approached the overpass and sounded his horn but no little old man appeared. Bob was disappointed to have missed his old friend but looked forward to giving his friendly wave on the way back. Hours passed and Bob stepped up into the locomotive and headed his long train back to the Tulsa station. As he approached the overpass he sounded long and hard on the train's horn but the little old man failed to appear. Bob literally stopped the train, stepped down from his high position of command and walked under the trestle and found his old friend had died during the night. He called the police.

Officers arrived, set up a perimeter and began the task of making reports and identifications. In the old man's wallet they found five dollars and an old driver's license bearing the name James Krispus. There were no photographs of family, no letters from friends, no indication where he came from or how he came to live under the trestle. No evidence that any one cared except for a train conductor who had endeared himself by a toot of the whistle and a wave of the hand.

Bullet: God often assigns someone to care even for the most unlikely. That someone could be a train conductor *or the reader of this book.*

Shield: "He who has a generous eye shall be blessed . . ." Proverbs 22:9 (NKJV)

Prayer: Lord, help me to understand that being my brother's keeper may mean nothing more than a watchful eye but to my brother it could be the eye of God.

55

Miss Geneva

Monday, June 7, 6:30 p.m.

Everyone called her Miss Geneva. A big lady, she sang in her church choir, taught Sunday school, and loved those grandbabies. Somehow, when her children grew up, they just got spread everywhere and Miss Geneva spent most of her summer months traveling the highways visiting them and those cute, adorable, smart, grandbabies. With two huge suitcases, a supply of assorted hats, and her almost new red Chrysler, she would set out on her summertime adventure.

Ken's life, on the other hand, was very different. Instead of grandbabies, his life evolved around search and seizure techniques, proper arrest procedures, and the endless lectures on officer safety. Time after time he was hammered by the statistics of officer fatalities during common traffic stops. "It's always the trusting good guys that get it," instructors would tell him. "Be considerate but be cautious. Be sure to go home to your family."

Little did these two people realize what would await them when their two worlds would meet each other. Miss Geneva didn't get started on her trip until late in the day. It was after midnight when she stopped at a small, bump-in-the-road market to get a cup of ice. She always carried soft drinks in the back seat. It was much cheaper that way. Miss Geneva paid for the cup of ice, thanked the attendant, and left.

She started the engine of her red Chrysler, turned onto the main highway, and twisted the cap off her soft drink so as to pour it in her cup of ice. As she replaced the cap and placed the soft drink bottle in the back seat, her eyes left the road. The big Chrysler eased onto the shoulder. She abruptly jerked it back into the center of the roadway and checked her rear view mirror. For hours she had been alone. Now there was a car behind her and it seemed to be speeding up as if to pass...but it didn't. It simply drew closer and was obviously following her.

Staring into her mirror with eyed widened and lucking her dry lips, Miss Geneva was afraid for the first time in a long time.

What did this stranger want? Would he harm her? What? Then the whole world seemed to fill itself with swirling red and blue lights. The revolving lights on the roof and alternating headlight beams on the vehicle behind her seemed to catapult her into another dimension. He COULDN'T be wanting her to stop. She was a grandmother for crying out loud! Miss Geneva slowed down but didn't stop. After all, there was no other traffic coming, he could pass. He surely didn't want HER to stop! The officer sounded his siren and Miss Geneva pulled onto the shoulder.

All alone in the patrol car, Ken thought of all the safety precautions. Help would be a long way off if he got in trouble. He had no idea who was in the vehicle in front of him or why they had refused to stop. Ken flipped on his "take down" lights, opened his driver's door, and directed the spotlight on the vehicle in front of him. Using his public address system he commanded the driver to "step outside and away from the vehicle."

Miss Geneva was livid! Not only had he frightened her, he was treating her like a common criminal! She sat in her seat, not wanting to obey his command, yet not knowing fully what to do. So she sat. Her short frame only allowed the officer to see a small portion of her head above the headrest of the Chrysler. Again he demanded that she exit the vehicle and step away. Only this time, he released the thumb break and eased the semi-automatic out of its holster. His palm was sweaty as he felt the coolness of the newly installed Pacmyer grips. His heart filled his ears with pulsating sounds yet he could hear a pin drop.

Slowly Miss Geneva got out of the car and asked, "Just WHAT do you think you're doing? I haven't done anything wrong and you treat me like a criminal with your bright lights, and your sirens, and your spotlights. I'M JUST A GRANDMOTHER!"

Ken sighed a sigh of relief and slid his gun back into the holster. He could have sent her on her way with little explanation and the whole event would send two people into the night feeling less about the world than when the night began. Instead, something very different took place. In the darkness of the night, with moths darting in and out of the bright lights, Ken took the extra few minutes to painstakingly explain his actions.

Trapped inside each of us are years of conceptions and misconceptions. The unfortunate thing about misconceptions is that, not only are they untruths, but they lead us to make false assumptions that birth both fear and fury. A police officer survives by expecting the worst. Yet, those very actions can offend those of us who try to live each day in a good, decent, and respectable manner. We want each officer to know us as "good citizens" on sight . . . an impossible task.

The explanation seemed to work. After a few minutes they were both able to chuckle about it. Each had shared a glimpse of how a person's learned behavior can shape their expectations. The officer bid her good evening and left.

Miss Geneva went on the find those grandbabies.

~⌣ ⌣⌢

Silver Bullet: Friends are often made only when we seek to understand someone other than ourselves.

Shield: "Discretion shall preserve thee, understanding shall keep thee." Proverbs 2:11

Prayer: Lord, help me to want to understand as strongly as I want to be right.

56

Let's Find Someone that Needs to Go to Jail....

Friday, October 8, 9:45 p.m.

He slid into the patrol car and with a boyish grin said, "Let's find someone that needs to go to jail and hope they don't want to go."

Only another cop would understand that statement. Nothing so truly defines the line drawn between good and evil, right and wrong, outlaw and lawman, like a good pursuit. For those moments in time, everything is on the line. The long arm of the law has been extended with its palm facing outward, and someone has blatantly, arrogantly, and intentionally defied that which is truth, justice, and the American way. It no longer matters what the person HAS done. It only matters what he IS doing. He is flagrantly stating, "I am untouchable. I am above the law, the badge means nothing to me."

Now the chase is on! Red and blue strobes alternately igniting make swirls of light bounce off the darkened city streets and buildings. The officer's voice loudly giving directions of travel into a radio microphone so as to be heard over the screams of his siren. Eyes trained to scan every intersection while remaining fastened on the vehicle attempting to elude you. He loves the sound of that beautiful engine down shifting automatically as he rounds the corners and roaring like a grandfather lion as it inhales more air to mix with the raw gas you're pumping down its throat. Yeah, this is good-guy bad-guy at its best.

But there was also another pursuit in progress. Not a good-guy bad-guy race, but a race of egos. Long hard weapons of steel, chariots of fire, sweeping toward a personal victory...the prize of escape vs. conquest ...courage vs. concern for safety. Are decisions now being driven by logic -- or the rush of emotional adrenaline? The officer has a wife and kids at home. Is this is a bad guy or a scared one? Is he a street-wise felon or a foolish kid?

The cop is lucky this time. The bad guy, in true form, believes he is better at this than he really is. He over compensates for a turn, loses control, and with a thundering sound of metal mashing against metal, glass shattering like an icicle on a frozen walkway, and billows of smoke and dust, it is over. The good guy wins.

Or does he?

Silver Bullet: Sometimes a value judgment cannot be made by all the facts. There are simply not enough of them. Instead, it has to be made with a clear head, looking into a clear conscious, for clear direction from a higher source.

Shield: Trust in the LORD with all your heart, and lean not on your own understanding. In all your ways acknowledge Him, and He shall direct your paths. Proverbs 3:5,6 (NKJV)

Prayer: Lord, I am Your gift to my community and my family. Help me to put aside my desire to prove myself to myself and listen to Your still small voice."

Manufactured By: RR Donnelley
                     Breinigsville, PA USA
                     December, 2010